Bell AH-1
Cobra

Bell AH-1
Cobra

Mike Verier

Published in 1990 by Osprey Publishing Limited
59 Grosvenor Street, London W1X 9DA

British Library Cataloguing in Publication Data
  Verier, Mike
  Bell AH-1 Cobra.
  1.   Military Helicopters to 1986
  I.   Title
  623.74'6047

ISBN 0–85045–934–6

Edited by Peter Gilchrist and Cathy Lowne
Printed and bound in Great Britain

FRONT COVER
*Carrying a formidable arsenal of weaponry beneath its stub
wings, an AH-1W sprayed up in standard Marine Corps
colours skims across the sea at speed*

TITLE PAGES
*The prototype Cobra, N209J, fitted up with an
experimental weapons suite, including an early version of
TOW* (Bell)

Contents

Acknowledgements

During the writing of this book, many people have generously given their time and expertise so that we may share their knowledge. It may sound rather clichéd, but there's no other way to say it—this history could not have been written without their help. Any mistakes are mine, of course, but I remain forever in the debt of all the people mentioned below, be it for information, photographs, bits of Cobra lore, or just plain old encouragement. Thank you one and all. My profound apologies, but no less gratitude, to anyone I have missed. In no special order then:

At Bell Helicopter, Bartram Kelly and Charles Seibel for interviews; Mr Seibel and Bob Duppstadt also kindly undertook to read and correct the original text, as did Dick Jarret who has been a staunch supporter of this project; thanks also to Jim and Babs Gooch for their support and hospitality; to Ted Hayes of the photographic department; Marty Reisch (now retired) and latterly Bob Leder of Public Affairs and not forgetting the long-suffering Lory Love. Special thanks to the paint shop for their very detailed assistance, and to countless other individuals who made my visits to Bell so enjoyable and informative.

Of the US Army, Lieutenant General Robert R Williams (retired), for adding considerably to the Army part of the story; Major Bruce Bell in Washington; Betty Goodson, Tom Greene and all the wonderful people at Fort Rucker; WO Russel Pace for a great deal of time and additional information; and again many Army personnel in numerous locations.

Of the US Marine Corps, Major Frank Batha (now retired) and the USMC Historical Center in Washington whose provision of very detailed historical documentation and general enthusiasm were the rock on which the second half of this book was founded. Through them I was able to correspond with, and eventually meet, Captain Peyton DeHart, who was a most patient correspondent in the face of a stream of obscure questions, and an excellent host during my subsequent visit to Camp Pendleton. Unbounded gratitude also to his wife Jayne for her hospitality to an itinerant British photographer!

Thanks also to the Public Affairs staff at MCAS New River, in particular Sergeant Cheryl North for her patience. Many other Marines smoothed my path and answered my questions; especially the officers and men of VMO-1, VMO-2, HMLA-169, HMLA-269 and HMLA-367. The last of these units, better known as 'Scarface', have graciously allowed this author to wear their insignia, an honour of which I am immeasurably proud. Thank you.

Many government agencies, including those of the US Army, the US Marine Corps, NASA, the US Customs Service, the US Air Force and US Navy have assisted with either information or guidance through the maze of clearances needed for a 'foreigner' to visit military installations. I hope the individuals involved will forgive my not listing them in detail, although one who deserves special mention is the redoubtable Richard Calder at the US Embassy's press office in London.

Acknowledgements are also due to my many friends and correspondents worldwide in the International Plastic Modellers' Society. It would be fair to say that their assistance has been fundamental and I can pay them no higher compliment than this book which is a tribute to their detailed research and dogged following of leads. Chief among these are Tom Kolk and Bryan Wilburn together with Brian Nicklas and the Washington DC Chapter, Aldo Zanfi of IPMS Italy—the original inspirer of this work—various editors of IPMS (UK) magazine, including Paul Beaver, the late and much-missed Bob Downey, Tim Laming and Neil Robinson. Others include Robin Howard and Robert C Knee.

Thanks also to Mr H W Foot and the staff at Middle Wallop's excellent Museum of Army Flying; the Editor and staff of the US Army Aviation Digest;

Major Fernando Cano Velasco of the Spanish Army; Bob Dorr, Lyn Sangster and, sadly, the late Bryan Philpott, not forgetting Dennis Baldry and Cathy Lowne of Osprey, and Peter Gilchrist.

Finally, thanks to Simon, Philip and my lovely wife Liz, who have endured far more than they should for the sake of this book.

Mike Verier
Canterbury, June 1989

Introduction

Warfare evokes many images, and surely one of the most enduring and powerful of these is sound. The aural image most of us have of World War 1, for instance, is the incessant rumble of artillery—a sort of dull, repetitive 'crump' as the background to almost any activity. From World War 2 we have the chilling sound of the Stuka dive-bomber, with its siren screaming as the aircraft makes a near-vertical attack on a defenceless city. The long and bitter conflict in Vietnam produced yet another unmistakable noise—that of the rhythmic, thudding beat of a massed helicopter assault.

How many people, I wonder, are aware that, to a very large extent, this characteristic sound is peculiar to one particular rotor system—that designed by Bell for the 'Huey' transport helicopter, and its combat offspring, the Cobra?

That the Cobra was born of the conflict in Vietnam is beyond question. Its overall history, however, began before the US involvement in SE Asia, and has extended for many years beyond it. Like many truly great warplanes before and since, the Cobra emerged in response to a particular military requirement, and subsequently proved itself capable of adapting to roles that were scarcely imagined at the time of its inception. The Cobra story currently spans the entire history of combat helicopters, and all dedicated attack types since, unless constrained by conversion from a utility airframe, have followed the same basic formula. It was a formula pioneered by the engineers at Bell, and it obviously works.

In making out a case for the Cobra to be included alongside such aviation greats as the Spitfire and Mustang, I can only say that any aircraft that has not only remained in front-line service, but also in production, for well over twenty years, is a remarkable machine. Add to that its enviable combat record in Vietnam, Grenada, the Lebanon, Israel and (probably) Iran, and you have the makings of a classic.

During the research for this book, it has been my privilege to talk to many of the people most closely associated with the aircraft, including designers, engineers, aircrew and maintenance personnel. Not once have I come across anyone with a bad word for the Cobra, and this has made the work of authorship hugely enjoyable and much easier than I first imagined. Consider the problems an author must face when 'optimistic' information from a manufacturer conflicts with the in-service actuality. Happily this was not the case with the Cobra, and wherever I looked I encountered the same kind of enthusiasm for what must be one of the most influential helicopters of our time. I hope, therefore, to convey some of that enthusiasm to you, the reader, so that this work will serve as a tribute to the aircraft itself, and to the people associated with it.

I should perhaps offer a word of explanation as to why the book is laid out the way it is. The chronology of the Cobra is a long and tortuous one. Starting at the AH-1G and working through to the AH-1W proved impracticable because so many programmes overlapped, or were developments of earlier variants. Fortunately there are two threads that run through the aircraft's history—parallel but very different paths along which its evolution can be charted quite distinctly.

The original Cobra was built to fill an obvious (though officially unrecognized) US Army requirement involving one particular conflict. The development of today's single-engined variants can therefore be traced back to 1958—or even earlier if you choose to go back to the first two-bladed rotor. The twin-engined variants, on the other hand, owe their existence to the US Marine Corps, which has continued to influence their development to this day. This particular part of the story has never been documented before, and I hope that some of the details included here will set the record straight.

Within the confines of a book like this, there will, inevitably, be areas covered in less detail than perhaps I would have liked. I have tried to maintain a reasonable balance, but make no apologies for the fact that I have spent a little more time on the uncharted corners of Cobra development, than on those parts of the story already explored at length by other authors.

Given that the Cobra is still very much in production and under active development, the definitive story of the aircraft is a long way from being written. Nevertheless, in setting down the history so far, I hope you will be able to share my conviction that the AH-1 truly deserves to be recognized as one of the more significant milestones in the unfolding story of aviation. It was, after all, the first helicopter in the world to carry the 'A' for Attack designation.

Chapter 1
Genesis

For almost as long as there have been flying machines, the eye of the military planner has lighted on the possibility of using them as weapons platforms. Frustrated in the early days by limited payload and performance, the fixed-wing aviator nevertheless finally succeeded in turning his mount into a viable offensive weapon, and during the course of two world wars aircraft assumed a highly significant role in combat—frequently proving the decisive edge to a campaign.

During the late 1930s and early 1940s the first practical helicopters began to emerge. These machines, with the obvious tactical advantage of vertical take-off and landing, clearly had an enormous potential on the battlefield, whether it be over land or at sea. However, the development of the helicopter was at least 20 years behind that of fixed-wing aircraft, and it was to be some time before real progress could be made towards a successful armed version. It also needed a very different kind of warfare to vindicate the concept.

The first recorded trials of a helicopter as a potential weapons platform go back as far as 1942 at the US Army's Wright Field, Ohio, when one of the Sikorsky XR4 prototypes was turned into a makeshift bomber by the simple expedient of the observer hefting a 25 lb practice bomb off his lap and over the side onto a chalked target some hundreds of feet below. From these somewhat crude beginnings, the tests went on to use a simple bomb rack complete with release mechanism, and a rudimentary bombsight. Whilst the practicality of the system was certainly proved, the idea of armed helicopters was thought to be little more than a novelty at the time because existing machines were far too slow and vulnerable to be of any real use in combat. Developments of the XR4, however, did enter production as the world's first purpose-designed military helicopters, and were used on both sides of the Atlantic for a variety of utility roles such as liaison, observation and rescue.

As helicopters developed and became more reliable, military operators began to re-examine their combat potential. During the Algerian conflict a French Army commander was credited with the destruction of a stubborn, hilltop-mounted rebel outpost, by using the casualty litters of an observation helicopter to carry aloft two soldiers with automatic weapons. The US Marines of HMM-361 also armed their UH-34Ds to give highly effective suppressive fire during Korean war operations. Both actions have been claimed as the real beginnings of the combat helicopter, but nobody can be completely sure about such distant events. As far as the United States was concerned, the most important single influence on the development of armed helicopters sprang from the historic 1947 National Security Act, which separated the US Air Force from its Army origins permanently.

The primary concern of the Air Force at that time was the possibility of global nuclear warfare. It was then believed that this was the only form a major war could take, and the Air Force devoted most of its energies to acquiring bombers and interceptors that flew ever higher and faster. The traditional ground-attack role—now known as close air support—was seen as an unnecessary adjunct to the real business of Air Force tasking, and it received a correspondingly low priority throughout the military and political funding structure. This change of attitude did not bother the US Marine Corps, which had its own integral support aircraft, but the Army was clearly going to have to find its own solution.

In 1955, Col Jay D Vanderpool, an Army officer with special operations experience in Korea and a confirmed advocate of the use of helicopters in battle, found himself posted to Fort Rucker in Alabama. Rucker was—and indeed still is—a huge training base. At the main entrance of the base today, a preserved UH-1 surmounts an imposing plinth that justiably carries a legend proclaiming Rucker to be: 'The home of Army aviation'.

The commander of the base at that time was Brig Gen Carl J Hutton. In June 1955 he instructed Vanderpool to begin investigations into the offensive use of helicopters. His excuse for this strictly unofficial move was a memorandum originating in the office of Gen Willard Wyman, which concerned the possible training of 'highly mobile' task forces. The memo did not actually suggest the use of helicopters, but then again, Hutton reasoned, neither did it say they should not be used.

Initially, Vanderpool began with a team of just five men, and they quickly discovered that there was very little existing data to work on. As early as 1950 Bell, in conjunction with the US Army, had experimentally mounted a bazooka anti-tank weapon on a Bell 47 (H-13), and there was also a certain amount of feedback from the French and USMC experiences (the Marines maintained a liaison officer at Rucker), but really it was a question of starting from scratch. The OH-13 was again chosen as the research vehicle—mainly because there were plenty available—and the aircraft was fitted with two .50 calibre machine guns and some slightly modified airborne anti-tank rockets. The reasoning behind the selection of .50 calibre guns was an assumption that if the airframe could cope with these, then lesser calibres would present no additional problems. The selection of unguided rockets was a logical one, based not only on the realization that an armed helicopter would need something heavier than machine guns, but on the simple fact that these weapons could be fired from a zero-travel launch rail that had virtually no weight penalty.

When everything was ready for the first static tests, the small knot of spectators who assembled on what is now the Matteson Range consisted only of Hutton, Vanderpool, the test crew and a very few others. A number of important questions needed answers. Would the muzzle blast of the guns shatter the bubble canopy of the OH-13? Would the rockets, which were designed for fixed-wing launch speeds in excess of 180 knots, tumble out of control at zero launch speed—even with the assistance of a 12 G shear-pin to delay release until peak power had been achieved?

The helicopter was firmly fixed to a platform for the initial tests. The guns were fired singly, then together, and in increasingly long bursts. To everyone's relief the huge plexiglass canopy remained intact (although on later tests the vibration did burst the canopy, and on one occasion the door came adrift and was riddled

Dating back to 1958, Bell's Model D 245 is the earliest known visualization of the Cobra concept. Note the wing-mounted mission equipment pods, and the obvious similarity to the Huey dynamics (Bell)

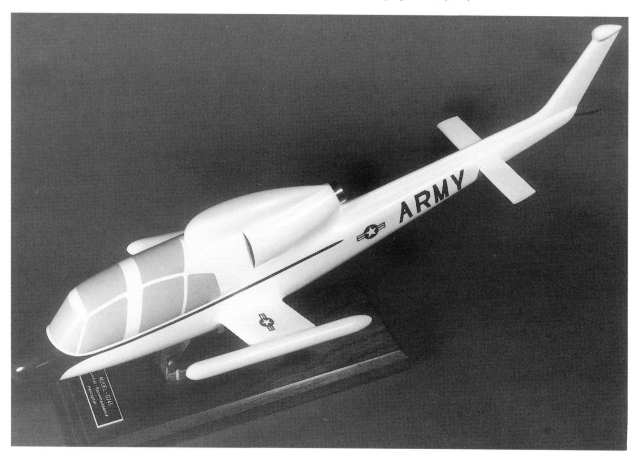

with gunfire!) The rockets were tried next. Again the firings were successful and, it was noted, surprisingly accurate. The aircraft was quickly reloaded and a second series of firings were conducted with the rotors turning and the pilot pulling some pitch on the blades to generate a good downwash. The OH-13 was still secured to the wooden platform, and again everything went smoothly. Finally the aircraft was unshackled and firings were completed from a low hover. It was now clear to everyone present that the sceptics had been wrong—using a helicopter as a weapons platform was not only possible but entirely practicable. The later problems with the plexiglass were easily resolved by 'soft' canopy mountings to isolate the vibration, and the doors were simply left off the aircraft to avoid the possibility of them shaking loose again. The small band of stalwarts who witnessed the first series of tests were, in the words of Col Vanderpool himself: 'a mighty excited and happy group'.

From these simple beginnings was to grow the airmobile concept, in which whole battalions are moved about the battlefield with previously undreamed of speed and mobility. The tacticians at Rucker first drew heavily on the tactics of the Duke of Wellington, who had developed the deployment of mounted infantry supported by mobile artillery and supply formations. The Rucker scenarios, with great foresight for the time, visualized an enemy equipped with radar and efficient anti-aircraft weapons, and the need for the helicopters to take advantage of whatever cover the terrain offered was recognized even at that early stage. Army pilots subsequently spent a great deal of time perfecting the technique of flying just above, or preferably between, the trees, in an early realization of what is now known as nap of the earth (NOE) flying. While the tactics and logistics of airmobile troops were being wrestled with on weekend exercises, the growing band of converts who were becoming known affectionately as 'Vanderpool's fools' were continuing to experiment with every conceivable form of armament. Just about anything that could be begged, borrowed or scrounged from other services or industry was tried, and despite the inevitable problems encountered along the way, a much wider understanding of helicopter armament began to emerge.

By this time interest was being shown at a much higher level. During 1957 the Marine Corps sent Lt Col Victor J Croizat and Maj David Riley to observe the French operations in Algeria. Their subsequent report went into great detail about the French Army's experience with a wide variety of weapons, and noted—with considerable interest from a USMC point of view—that the French regarded armed helicopters as an ideal means of protecting their transport elements, and of providing a 'highly flexible base of fire in support of ground elements', at least until the ground forces were well enough established to protect themselves. It was also significant that in

1957 Bell fitted the French SS-11 wire-guided anti-tank missile to an OH-13, and another experiment had seen the installation of a surplus B-29 turret under the nose of a Piasecki CH-21. This ex bomber turret was far too heavy to be practical, but the advantages of a trainable weapon were not lost on those concerned.

All of this experimentation was only of limited value to the piston-engined helicopters of the 1950s, but a virtual revolution in design was close at hand. In October 1956 Bell had flown the first turbine-engined XH-40. This aircraft, which would initially carry the service designation HU-1 (and ever after the affectionate name of 'Huey'—despite a later change of designation to UH-1 and its official name of 'Iroquois'), represented a huge leap in performance, the much lighter and more powerful turbine powerplant at last conferring a useful load capability on the helicopter. Even before the first production example of the HU-1A reached US Army service in 1959, there was a new design model at the Fort Worth headquarters of Bell Helicopter, representing Project D 245. It was referred to as the Combat Reconnaissance Helicopter, and although it was clearly based on Huey components, it featured a slender, tandem-seated cockpit and stub wings . . . the Cobra was coming.

As noted earlier, the US Marine Corps had not been idle during this period. An experimental team had test fired the French SS-11 missile from a UH-34D, and the subsequent report saw 'no difficulty' in using these or Zuni ballistic rockets from helicopters. Other tests considered various guns and rockets, culminating in the successful firing by Capt Samuel J Fulton of the Bullpup command-guided air-to-surface missile from a UH-34 in the summer of 1960. Despite a number of successful firings, the helicopter-launched Bullpup programme was not continued, although modern equivalent combinations such as the helicopter-launched Exocet are now seen as formidable weapons systems.

Despite enthusiastic testing, the USMC in general continued to regard the armed helicopter with a very low level of interest. The Marines naturally kept a close eye on developments at Rucker, but their requirements were fundamentally different because they operated a significant force of fixed-wing combat aircraft. The Army was prohibited from using its fixed-wing support aircraft in any armed role, and was therefore totally committed to helicopters.

In May 1959 the first American advisers were sent to South Vietnam to help the Government resist minor guerilla incursions from the communist North. Only two months later, on 8 July, the US group suffered its first casualties when several men were wounded during an attack on Bien Hoa. By May 1960 the personnel strength of the Military Assistance Advisory Group (MAAG) had risen from 327 to 685.

During 1960, with research and development funds

now available and the HU-1 beginning to appear on the inventory, the Army began to capitalize on its earlier experiments and try out the airmobile 'sky cavalry' concept for real. By this time command at Rucker had been passed to Gen Bogardus S Cairns. When the time came to compile hastily a tactics manual for the new formations, it was this ex cavalry officer who managed to track down a copy of the last field manual issued to US horse soldiers. This 1936 vintage document was heavily plagiarized by the authors of the new publication; the tactics of battle were still perfectly valid, although the method of transport had changed beyond all recognition.

That same year, with US Secretary of Defense, Robert McNamara, calling for greater mobility within the Army, Gen Hamilton H Howze took the chair of the Army Tactical Mobility Requirements Board at Fort Bragg. The 'Howze Board', as it became known, was later to issue a report that would shape the future of Army aviation and set in motion the train of events that would lead directly to the appearance of the Cobra.

Howze formalized the concepts proposed by the pioneers at Rucker. Army aviation was to be built around the Air Assault Division, in which helicopters would completely replace surface transport. This was to lead to the formation of the 1st Cavalry Division (Airmobile), which would deploy to Vietnam to test the validity of the concept in battle. The Board made a

string of further recommendations, ranging from the suitability of various weapons for different types of aircraft, to the identification of a clear requirement for an armed escort helicopter. The escort was needed to provide suppressive fire to the main formation during transits over hostile territory, and in the immediate vicinity of the landing zone (LZ).

To meet this requirement, it was advised that a percentage of UH-1s be armed to act in the escort role. Bell, of course, had arrived at similar conclusions some time before. Company engineers and technical people were already serving alongside Army personnel wherever the new Iroquois was deployed, and they were getting firsthand information—not from a bunch of 'Washington Warriors', but from the men at the front line who were working with the machine. The continual feedback from active service units was the stuff that really mattered, and this information would not be wasted.

The 'Slick' Hueys in Vietnam were basically transport helicopters, but they were armed with two pintle-mounted M-60 machine guns to provide a limited degree of protection over and around the landing zone. Note the upturned 'anti-Strella' exhaust, flak vests and armoured seats for the crew, and the wearing of personal side-arms—all vital precautions in any war zone (Museum of Army Flying via Mike Verier)

LEFT
The 'Hog' armament system is seen here on the UH-1B gate-guard at Fort Rucker. The XM-3 pods each held 24 2.75 inch FFARs, and the combined weight of a fully loaded system was well in excess of 1400 lb. This weight, added to that of the crew and a full load of fuel, gave the engine and transmission a hard time at take-off. The combination's reluctance to get airborne gave the XM-3 equipped aircraft its 'Hog' nickname (Mike Verier)

BELOW
The first full-scale mock-up of Project D 255 was unveiled in June 1962. It carried a streamlined 20 mm gun under the fuselage and a turreted grenade-launcher in the nose (Bell)

ABOVE
The gunner's pantograph-mounted sighting mechanism is evident in this picture of the mock-up. The US military designation and 'serial' were wishful thinking at that time, and even the Iroquois Warrior name didn't last too long. Note the pilot sitting well above the gunner, and the 1960s-style 'motorcycle' helmets (Bell)

LEFT
The D 255 mock-up was later shown with models of SS-11 type anti-tank missiles under one of the stub wings (Bell).

In early 1962 the arrival of two additional Army aviation units in Vietnam brought American military strength there up to some 4000. It was to prove an eventful year for Bell Helicopter. Company reps were also serving in SE Asia by then, and field modifications for the various Huey models were flowing in thick and fast. Eventually three distinct forms of the standard UH-1 were to evolve, each one known by a singularly American appellation that signified its armament and role. The basic Huey would become a 'Slick'—which meant that it was essentially a troop-carrier, with a 7.62 mm M60 machine gun in each doorway (the mountings for which were often no more complicated than a 'bungee' cord arrangement suspended from the roof). The proper armed Hueys featured a cross-fuselage mounting beam that protruded from each side of the cabin to provide hard-points for various combinations of guns and rockets. If the aircraft was to be used in an 'artillery' role, it could carry two 24-round pods of 2.75 inch forward-firing aerial rockets (FFARs), and as such was known as a 'Hog'. In the more general fire-suppression role, the weapons were mixed and consisted of two pairs of M60s or two multi-barrelled M21 Miniguns mounted outboard, and two seven-shot (or sometimes 19-shot) FFAR pods inboard. These aircraft were known to every infantryman as 'Cobras'.

In the midst of a massive production programme for the UH-1, Bell's development people had not been idle. They were convinced that sooner or later the Army would need a dedicated combat helicopter. Modified Hueys were undoubtedly doing a good job, but adding all the armament slowed the aircraft down to some 74–82 knots (depending on load), compared with the 85–90 knots of a troop-carrying Slick. This had the effect of slowing the whole escorted formation down, and thereby increasing its time of exposure to

enemy fire. The company's initial answer to the problem was Project D 255, a full-scale mock-up of which was unveiled in June 1962.

Better known as the Iroquois Warrior, D 255 revealed for the first time many of the features that were to become definitive for attack helicopters. The crew of two were seated in tandem under a canopy that offered exceptional all-round vision. The pilot in the rear seat was slightly raised so that his forward view was unimpaired, and the gunner was placed in the extreme nose. Stub wings had six hard-points for a variety of weapons, and the aircraft carried a 20 mm machine-gun in a faired belly pod and a turreted grenade-launcher in the nose. In order to solve the aiming problems of a remote turret, it was slaved to the gunner's sight, which was mounted on a pantograph arrangement to give him ample freedom of movement throughout the weapon's arc of fire. Pictures of the Warrior show clearly how much the airframe had in common with the basic UH-1. This made good commercial sense to Bell, but it also pleased the politicians, who were becoming increasingly attracted to commonality of equipment.

The Army people who saw the Warrior mock-up were impressed, but the whole concept had to be proved on something more conclusive than paper. During December 1962 Bell engineers began the modification of an OH-13 airframe, which was later to emerge as the Model 207 Sioux Scout. The Scout was

never intended as anything more than a proof-of-concept vehicle; it was too seriously underpowered for any consideration in a combat role, but it was able to demonstrate decisively that the company was working along the right lines. The original bubble canopy of the OH-13 was replaced by a lean, tandem cockpit for the crew of two, with the gunner seated forward of, and slightly below, the pilot. The aircraft was armed with a turreted pair of M-60 machine guns beneath the nose, operated through a pantograph sighting system similar to that first seen on Project D 255. Because the sight and its mounting occupied the space where the cyclic stick would normally be, Bell engineers installed novel side-arm controllers in the front cockpit to give the gunner a full set of flight controls. This was quite revolutionary for the time,

but it proved to be entirely practical. Stub wings were mounted in a shoulder position aft of the canopy, primarily to improve stability and augment lift, but the little prototype did carry a few rockets on them at times—just to reinforce the point about weapons capability.

The Scout was first flown in July 1963 and Bell lost no time in evaluating its potential, as well as demonstrating it to as many interested parties as possible. The general reaction was entirely favourable. The aircraft was considerably more manoeuvrable than the original OH-13 airframe, and all the new features seemed to work out well. In January 1964 it was turned over to the 11th Air Assault Division for a thorough military evaluation, and the test report recommended that a scaled-up version should be developed forthwith. This is just what the people from Fort Worth wanted to hear.

Secretary of Defense, Robert McNamara, announced on 15 November 1963 that US involvement in SE Asia would be over, 'by the end of 1965', and accordingly it was proposed that 1000 US personnel (out of a total of 15,000 at that time) would be withdrawn by early December. Just seven days later President John F Kennedy was assassinated in Dallas, and a visibly shocked Vice President, Lyndon B Johnson, found himself catapulted into the Oval Office as Commander-in-Chief of the United States Armed Forces. The political upheavals that followed Kennedy's death had the effect of reversing the policy of withdrawal from Vietnam, and by December 1965 over 180,000 US troops were stationed in SE Asia.

At about the time the US Army was evaluating the Sioux Scout, Bell Helicopter's President, E J Ducayet, was touring the active war zone with a team of engineers, interviewing service personnel and the resident Bell technicians, in order to ascertain more clearly the operational features an attack helicopter would need. The company saw the visit as vital, because it allowed a much more direct understanding of the Army requirement. During the course of the tour preliminary designs were shown to Gen Seneff (an ardent exponent of the armed helicopter, who would eventually be credited with the Cobra's first 'kill'), and to Gen Westmoreland, whose immediate reaction was essentially 'great, but no good unless you can have them here within two years'. That, the men from Bell thought, would be tough, but not impossible.

AAFSS

By the middle of 1964 the US Army had decided that it *did* need a dedicated weapons helicopter. The formal request for proposals (RFP) issued in August that year called for competing companies to tender for a long-range, very comprehensively equipped, deep interdiction aircraft. Whilst the RFP did not actually

ABOVE
The prototype Cobra is seen here with its undercarriage retracted, and is finished in a smart promotional camouflage scheme. The ventral fin was removed very early in its career (Bell)

RIGHT
N209J was used for many experimental programmes before its final retirement. It is seen here at Fort Worth in June 1969, equipped with an enlarged ammunition bay (immediately aft of the turret) and an early TOW launcher (Bell)

specify a helicopter, the very ambitious design goals made it almost certain that the Advanced Aerial Fire Support System (known by its acronym, AAFSS, pronounced 'Ayfuss') would certainly not be a fixed-wing type. Seven rival manufacturers—including Bell—tendered for the contract, but it was clear that the winning design could not be operational for some years, because the combination of so many advanced features would need a considerable development period. The engineers at Bell knew that the troops in Vietnam needed an effective aircraft quickly, and furthermore, the company was confident that it could be built within a sensible timescale. The 1965 New Year edition of *Bell News* looked forward to a successful business year, and after reporting on the achievements of existing products, an editorial spoke of ideas that were still 'under wraps'. The management had already decided to go ahead with a new turbine-engined project—the Model 209—as a purely company-funded venture.

Even as the AAFSS competition was running, the Army had begun to realize that a more modest and attainable machine was needed. A committee was formed, under the chairmanship of Col H L Bush, to examine the possibility of adapting an existing type to meet an 'interim' requirement, rather than waiting until the projected 1970 arrival time of the more advanced AAFSS. The 'Bush Board' considered four types: armed versions of the Sikorsky Sea King, Boeing-Vertol Chinook and Kaman Seasprite, and Bell's projected Model 209—which,

they were assured, was simply a modified UH-1. The modified UH-1B proposed by Bell could, they suggested, be procured quickly and at low cost—possibly even substituted for conventional Huey gunships already on order. Furthermore, due to the high degree of commonality between the two types, the Army could expect minimum impact on its training and logistics organizations.

On 7 September 1965, just two days after its roll-out, the 209 had a successful first flight. The as yet unbuilt Lockheed AH-56 Cheyenne helicopter was declared the winner of the AAFSS competition in November 1965, but by that time the Cobra had already demonstrated a top speed of around 175 knots—well in excess of the existing world record for its class. Subsequent fly-offs between the Cobra and the other three 'Bush Board' types at Edwards AFB, amply confirmed its wide-ranging superiority.

On Thursday, 7 April 1966, a $2.7 million development contract was issued by the US Army Aviation Material Command for the design, production and qualification-testing of two prototype UH-1H aircraft. Six days later a further contract worth $20.5 million was issued calling for 110 production units of the new helicopter. The Cobra had arrived.

Chapter 2
Snake Hatch

The development of a privately funded prototype is never undertaken lightly, especially when the aircraft concerned is aimed at a military requirement that does not officially exist. The US Army's need for an armed escort helicopter had been enshrined in the ambitious AAFSS programme during the summer of 1964, but the management team at Bell was convinced that the emphasis of the published requirement was seriously flawed. The company had been closely monitoring the front-line requirements for a weapons-carrying helicopter in SE Asia for some time, and had formed a very clear idea of the shape, size and performance standards needed by the aircraft, which was still primarily regarded as an armed scout.

Despite its misgivings, the company had submitted a proposal, Model D 262, against the AAFSS requirement in November 1964. Earlier that year, almost simultaneously with the arrival of the AAFSS RFP documentation, Bell engineers had started tentative internal discussions about the feasibility of building an aircraft that would meet *their* understanding of the Army's requirement, paying particular attention to the time factors involved. The rationale for even considering this expensive proposition was simple: AAFSS would have to be a large, high-performance and technologically advanced machine, certainly needing some form of compounding (a blend of helicopter and fixed-wing technologies) to meet the demanding specification which was way beyond that of a pure helicopter. Such a machine could certainly be built, but it would be a high-risk programme and need a considerable period of development. The final AAFSS production machine would also cost a great deal more than the simpler armed scout helicopter, which would possibly restrict its eventual service use to relatively small numbers.

Following submission of the D 262 proposal, Bell suspected at a fairly early stage that the design would not win the AAFSS contract. This was confirmed

during the spring of 1965 when the original seven contenders were reduced to just two—Lockheed and Sikorsky. Both of these companies went on to complete a government-funded, six-month project definition phase, before the Lockheed design was finally selected for full-scale development. When the Bell Corporation was officially told that D 262 had been rejected, a decision was taken to build a scout prototype—the formal go-ahead being agreed during a meeting held in early March 1965.

This was the precise point at which the Model 209 was conceived. Had Bell won the AAFSS competition there would not have been a Cobra.

The fundamental problem that remained was one of time. Could a process that normally takes at least 18 months be condensed into a period of only six? And if so, could the project be held to a budget of only $1 million—an amount that would hardly buy a new weapons rack today, let alone a whole new aircraft! The fact that the company's engineers succeeded so well is a remarkable testimony to their skill and determination.

A secure 'green room' was quickly built in the Experimental Department's hangar at Fort Worth, under the auspices of the shop superintendent, 'Red' Woodall. The design staff set to work immediately, with Charles Seibel as chief experimental projects engineer, assisted by Bob Duppstadt, and Mike Folse. They rapidly assembled a team around them that at its peak included 42 engineers, supported by a further 17 staff from other departments. Duppstadt recalls that *esprit de corps* was very high, and a close

The tandem seating arrangement gives the Cobra its very slim frontal area, making it a difficult target to knock down. Here N209J is seen with early rocket pods. The frangible fairings are to aid streamlining. (Bell)

relationship developed with the company management. Morning visits by Bell's President, E J Ducayet, became an almost daily ritual, and it was he who hung Owen Day's *Nobody loves a fat boy* poster on the green room wall to remind everybody how critical the weight of the aircraft would be.

By August 1965 construction of the prototype was sufficiently far advanced for Bell to present the 'modified UH-1' to the Bush Board as a firm contender for the interim escort type they were seeking. Only a month later the first example of this new breed of helicopter was flying, carrying the specially reserved US civil registration N209J to reflect its company model number. The rest, of course, is history.

Design Considerations

Given that Bell saw little need for speeds in excess of 175 knots for the kind of armed scout helicopter envisaged, the new design completely eliminated most of the problems that were later to bedevil the 250 knot AH-56. In a 1967 paper delivered to the American Helicopter Society, Charles Seibel was able to show that below 200 knots the pure helicopter was just fine, but anything more adventurous than that could run into all sorts of difficulties—especially with the rotor-blade technology of the mid 1960s.

The overall length of the Model 209 was dictated by the need to use UH-1 dynamic components, and the design of the tandem-cockpit/nose-turret configuration produced the basic three foot wide fuselage that remains unchanged today. The much smaller airframe had to hold additional fuel (for increased loiter time), and carry virtually the same avionics package as a standard Huey, but it also had to carry more weapons and have much better maintenance access. Initially a monocoque structure was considered, but this was discarded because the rigid panels gave poor access. A box-beam and honeycomb-panel construction was eventually chosen in order to provide the necessary airframe stiffness, and this left ample scope in the resultant semi monocoque fuselage for non-structural panels that could be removed for easy servicing.

To reduce drag as much as possible, an unusual degree of attention was paid to the aerodynamics of the new helicopter. Fuselage lines were carefully designed to avoid stalled areas, and all the rivets and screws used in the forward fuselage were flush fitting. The antennas were either flush mounted or fully submerged, and all the internal drain channels were 'ganged' to minimize the number of exit apertures—this last point accounting for the comparatively oil-free undersides of in-service Cobras! The unavoidably stalled area aft of the mast and pitch links was aerodynamically isolated from the pylon by a so-called 'surfboard' fairing, thus preventing stall precipitation of the pylon itself. On early aircraft, drag was reduced even more by using a mast-mounted spinner-plate to seal the opening in the top of the pylon. The stub wings, primarily fitted to support weapons, were also streamlined, further reducing drag and even marginally contributing to lift at high speeds.

A useful reduction in the overall frontal area of the aircraft was achieved by designing semi flush intakes which 'inhaled' ample air from the fuselage boundary layer to feed the single Lycoming T53-L-13 engine. The exhaust gases were directed aft and slightly upwards—an arrangement that provided some additional thrust, but also made it more difficult for ground-based infra-red seeking weapons to lock on to the hot end of the turbine.

The prototype was built—and flew throughout its life—with a retractable skid undercarriage. This was done to allow a number of aerodynamic and operational trade-offs to be assessed. Obviously streamlining was a considerable benefit of the retraction system, and it was also felt that a greater turret arc would be possible with the skids out of the way. On the other side of the equation were the extra weight and complexity of the system, the crashworthiness of a combat-damaged aircraft, and such mundane considerations as the inevitability of an average service pilot failing to remember that the undercarriage was not 'down and welded'.

Testing quickly established that there would be no particular problems with a fixed-skid configuration. The turret could not practicably be traversed that far backwards anyway, and full weapons release (with suitable sequencing and outboard impetus in the event of emergency jettison) was found to be possible with the skids in position throughout the entire flight envelope of the aircraft itself. The extra weight of the retraction system was therefore discarded, and all production aircraft were fitted with an aerodynamically improved, fixed landing gear.

Similar trade-off considerations accompanied the deletion from production aircraft of the prototype's armoured glass windscreen. It had been calculated that the chance of a direct hit in that area was only four per cent, and this was considered not enough to justify the extra weight penalty. The decision was

ABOVE RIGHT
The Cobra was designed for trouble-free maintenance in the field, and is equipped with a large number of access panels. This early Vietnam picture shows the primitive working conditions endured by the ground crews (Museum of Army Flying via Mike Verier)

RIGHT
The fourth production AH-1G (615249), pictured here immediately after delivery, shows the clean lines of the fuselage and the semi flush intakes. The 'surfboard' fairing at the top of the pylon isolates the turbulence caused by the rotating shaft and pitch-links (US Army Aviation Digest via Mike Verier)

LEFT
The Cobra's exhaust is directed slightly upwards, but it still makes an inviting target for modern heat-seeking missiles (US Army Aviation Digest via Mike Verier)

BELOW LEFT
The prototype was built with a retractable undercarriage, but for a variety of reasons this was not carried through onto production aircraft. Seen here at the beginning of 1969, the aircraft is fitted with an experimental weapons kit, including an early TOW system. Note the company 'gunner' using his telescopic sight unit (Bell)

BELOW
Although Bell's standard Model 540 rotor was fitted to production aircraft, an experimental power folding system was tried during 1972. This would have made the Cobra easier to transport and conceal, but the extra weight and complexity of the system was not considered worthwhile (Bell)

not seen in quite the same light by those who spent 100 per cent of their time in the four per cent zone, and sadly, as if to emphasize the point, one of the earliest combat casualties was hit between the eyes by a .50 calibre bullet. Nevertheless, the armoured glass was not retained. Subsequent combat experience was to prove that the chances of an adversary even *attempting* to fire at a heavily armed Cobra, particularly one that was pointing straight at him, were understandably low.

The 27-inch chord rotor and dynamics of the UH-1C were applied to the Cobra almost unchanged. Bell's classic and well proven 'door hinge' (Model 540) two-bladed rotor was found to be ideal for the job. It was tough and durable, with ample strength to absorb considerable combat damage. A twin-bladed rotor is less costly to produce and service than a unit with four blades, as well as being easier to stow and less susceptible to gusts—particularly during staring-up. The 540 rotor rendered the aircraft highly responsive in manoeuvre and perfectly controllable if kept within positive G. The aircraft is capable of aerobatic manoeuvres, and some pilots have survived loops and rolls in a Cobra. However, this kind of aerodynamic abuse does bring the aircraft dangerously close to the edge of its flight envelope, and is not recommended to pilots who aspire to old age!

The one significant change to the rotor system was the deletion of the standard Huey's stabilizer bar— again to save weight and reduce drag. This necessi-

tated the introduction of an electronic stability control augmentation system (SCAS), which was arranged in such a manner that external disturbances were heavily damped while pilot inputs received a quick and positive response. The SCAS control laws took some time to perfect, but ultimately the system worked so well that Cobra drivers to a man still say that the aircraft is a delight to fly.

Early in the Cobra programme a certain amount of difficulty was experienced with the yaw stability of the aircraft, and this persisted for some time. The prototype was originally flown with a substantial ventral fin to provide stability in autorotation, similar to that later found on the KingCobra. This was deleted at an early stage, but the yaw problem remained. At one stage NASA even schemed a 'butterfly' or V-tail unit for the AH-I, but the solution eventually adopted was to move the tail rotor from the port side of the fin to starboard.

The cockpit design for the Model 209 closely followed the pattern originally shown in mock-up form on the Iroquois Warrior, and later tested on the Sioux Scout. The gunner was seated at the front, with a pantograph-mounted sight which afforded him maximum freedom of movement to ensure high target acquisition rates. He was also provided with basic flight instruments and side-arm controls to enable him to act as co-pilot.

The command pilot was seated behind and above the gunner in order to maintain adequate vision. He was provided with a full flight instrumentation and avionics package, and conventional (not helicopter) cyclic and collective controls. The coaming of the rear instrument panel was surmounted by a reflector-type sighting system to enable the pilot to aim and fire the wing-mounted stores. The turret gun could also be fired by the pilot, but only when it was in the stowed (straight ahead) position.

The crew were housed in a virtually unobstructed 'greenhouse' canopy which offered outstanding vision in all directions. Both seats were lightly armoured, and additional Ausform armour plates could be raised on each side of the crewmen to provide extra protection against small arms fire. It was quickly discovered that the large, clear canopy created unpleasant 'hothouse' conditions for the crew, and

effective air-conditioning became an essential. An engine-driven fan was installed to supply ventilation not only to the cockpit area in general, but also to both crew seats, making them some of the most comfortable that pilots will encounter. A final addition to the creature comforts of the Cobra—only recently deleted—were the ash trays provided in each cockpit of the production aircraft!

Armament

The primary purpose of the Model 209 was to carry weapons. The basic design featured two hardpoints on each stub wing, and all four could support either a seven-round (XM-157) or 19-round (XM-159) rocket pod, housing 2.75 inch FFARs. As an alternative, the inboard racks only could accommodate an M-18E1 six-barrelled 7.62 mm Minigun pod, complete with 1500 rounds of ammunition.

The production Cobra was always intended to have the XM-28 dual-weapon turret in the nose, but its limited availability meant that early aircraft were fitted with the Emerson Electric TAT-102A—a modified version of the turret designed for USMC UH-1s. The TAT-102A housed a single GAU-2B/A six-barrelled 7.62 mm Minigun, which was provided with 4000 rounds of ammunition fed from a bay immediately aft of the turret. For ease of access the large doors into the ammunition bay opened on both sides of the fuselage, and were stressed to double as servicing platforms.

The later XM-28 turret was to prove a formidable device. Each one could hold two weapons—the GAU-2B/A Minigun and the XM-129 40 mm grenade launcher—either as a pair or in combination, depending on the mission requirements. As the gunner sat directly over the chin turret, he not only had a very real 'fire-hose' sense of weapon direction, but his line of sight intersected the ballistic trajectory of 7.62 mm ammunition twice over a range of 800 m, giving him a very high probability of hitting the target with the first burst.

The turret itself could be trained over a 230 degree arc of fire, and depressed 60 degrees below datum or elevated to 25 degrees. This meant that a considerable

The Cobra's fighter-type canopy offers superb vision to both crew members, but the 'greenhouse effect' was difficult to live with. Here the prototype (foreground) formates with the first two production aircraft. Minor development differences between the three are already visible (Bell)

ABOVE
One of the US Army's AH-1Gs being re-armed during the Vietnam conflict. The 19-shot XM-159 rocket pod on the inner station is being loaded, while the outer station holds an XM-157 seven-shot pod. Note the open access door to the ammunition bay, and the 4000-round drum-like magazine for the turreted GAU-28/A Minigun (Museum of Army Flying via Mike Verier)

swathe of territory either side of the aircraft flight path could be 'suppressed', even during an attacking run using the wing-mounted stores. For target marking, provision was made for smoke grenades and flares to be carried in the rear fuselage. The magazine for these markers hinged downwards, so that any grenade dropped during loading would fall outside the airframe.

Selling the Snake

The marketing people at Bell always liked the name Cobra for their new helicopter, and were reluctant to adopt the normal US Army practice of naming the aircraft after an Indian tribe. It might be thought that the name was selected to provide a link with the P-39 Airacobra and P-63 Kingcobra, both of which were built in large numbers by the company during the 1940s. In fact this was only partly the case.

During the early 1960s the company had forged strong links with all the UH-1 units serving in SE Asia, most of which had colourful titles such as *Soc Trang Tigers, Mavericks, Playboys*, etc. The first UH-1 unit to be deployed directly from the United States to Vietnam (in April 1963) was the 114th Airmobile Company, whose 'guns'—the new UH-1B gunship helicopters—quickly became known as the *Vinh Long Cobras*. It was this unit that lent its name unofficially to all the gunship versions of the UH-1, and consequently to Bell's scout helicopter proposal, which was originally referred to as the UH-1 Cobra.

This rather provisional name was to find its final form as the result of a suggestion by Gen 'Ham' Howze, who had retired from the Army by then and was working for Bell. Everyone knew that the UH-1 designation and official Indian name of 'Iroquois' were largely ignored throughout the Army, and wherever Bell's popular transport helicopter served it was simply known as a 'Huey'. Gen Howze pointed out that the name HueyCobra had a nice ring to it in relation to the Model 209. When Bell consulted the dictionary they found a description of the Cobra that referred to it as 'a snake that resides in Far Eastern climes, that can detect its enemy visually or by sensing

body heat (FLIR ?), and strike quickly, spitting venom with deadly accuracy', they were completely sold, and HueyCobra was formally accepted as the company name for the helicopter.

Army bureaucracy was not so convinced however, and did not give up that easily. The order for the first two aircraft quoted the designation UH-1H. A modification to the contract followed on 19 May 1966, officially changing the designation to AH-1G (meaning Attack Helicopter, with 'G' as the next available letter in the H-1 series). At the time the Army was also 'experiencing some legal difficulties' with Piper, who were also naming their aircraft after American Indian tribes, and another change to the contract on 13 July finally recognized the new aircraft as the 'AH-1G (Cobra)'—a resigned acceptance of defeat in reality, and no alternative name has ever been seriously suggested.

The Bell sales people have never been averse to a little 'showbiz' as a selling aid, and confirmation of the name Cobra presented them with an ideal opportunity. The attention-getter comes in a variety of forms, some more serious than others, but Joe Mashman (then Vice President in charge of market development) firmly believed that if you could make them laugh, the sale was already half completed. The prototype aircraft was a prime example of this sense of fun. For some time the co-pilot's collective lever was surmounted by a real Cobra head during exhibitions and demonstrations. Mashman would carefully remove this each night, and place it in its own polished mahogany case. The head was presented to the company by Lawrence Curtis and J P Jones, curators of Fort Worth's Forest Park Zoo. Mashman had originally asked for a King Cobra's head, but this was deemed 'much too large, and not near pretty enough' by Curtis and Jones, so a Spectacle Cobra was used instead. This change in the specification even caused an appropriate amendment to engineering order 209A220! Sadly, the original snake's head was reported 'mislaid' in Munich during the aircraft's 1967 European tour. The Cobra message however, was still amply reinforced by a supply of realistic rubber snakes which were always available during the early marketing exercise. Suitably sprung on an unsuspecting briefee, these were reputed to ensure his undivided attention during presentation of the new aircraft!

LEFT
The head of a Spectacle Cobra was specially modified to fit over the co-pilot's collective lever N209J, near the 'panic button', which was unique to this prototype (Bell)

ABOVE RIGHT
The original Engineering Order specified a King Cobra head—but an amendment was issued later (Bob Duppstadt)

Prototype Postscript

The prototype Cobra (N209J) served the development and sales programme for nearly six years. It assisted in qualification work for a wide range of weapons and systems, toured America and Europe giving demonstrations to US Forces and other potential customers, and was heavily involved in a diversity of flight-test programmes. Finally deactivated in 1971, it was restored to its original configuration, and since November 1972 has rested in honourable retirement at the General George S Patton Museum, Fort Knox.

In correspondence with the author, Cobra designer 'Charlie' Siebel mentioned that a second experimental Cobra was built to do the weapons qualification. The wing structure of N209J was not adequate to support *all* the weapons required by the Army. This aircraft was identical to N209J except for its stronger wing and the deletion of the retractable landing gear, which was fixed in the extended position and streamlined.

Chapter 3
Early Years

Following the obvious success of the prototype (N209J), the US Army awarded Bell a $2.7 million contract for two more Cobras, built to production standards for a qualification and testing programme. Ordered on 7 April 1966, these two aircraft (67-7015 and 67-7016) were essentially the first AH-1Gs. Only a matter of days later, an initial batch of 110 Cobras was ordered—the first true production aircraft.

As the tempo of production built up, the urgency of early deployment was in everybody's thoughts, and the training of Army aircrew and ground personnel began as soon as sufficient aircraft were available. On 30 September 1966, the Army ordered seven systems trainers (non-flying airframes for maintenance and systems instruction), and another 210 AH-1G models were ordered on 30 November. A third big production order brought the total procurement up to 530 aircraft by March 1967.

While the Cobra was engaged in its two-phase qualification and testing programme at Fort Hood, preparations for deployment were well in hand. During May 1967 a New Equipment Training Team (NETT) was formed around the aircraft, under the command of Lt Col Paul Anderson. The unit's primary responsibilities were the introduction of the Cobra into SE Asia, the development of tactics, and the conversion of operational units onto the aircraft. The organization was staffed by some of the most experienced aircrew in the Army.

The prototype was very well received at the Paris Salon in 1967, while back home at Fort Worth the production facilities were getting into top gear to enable the Army to start operational flying as quickly as possible. On 29 August Anderson's NETT unit was airlifted into Bien Hoa, and within two days of their arrival the first AH-1Gs had appeared in the skies over Vietnam.

First blood for the Cobra was claimed remarkably quickly. On 4 September 1967 Maj Gen George

Seneff, a long-time proponent of the gunship concept, destroyed a hostile sampan during what was supposed to be an 'introductory' flight: four Vietcong were killed in the attack. Two days later, a $60 million order added another 214 Cobras to the Army requirement.

The staff of the NETT organization settled into the routine task of teaching people to handle the Cobra. Although officially a training formation, their tactics brief encouraged them to engage the enemy whenever possible, and they quickly secured clearance to operate in 'War Zone D'. This was a designated free-fire zone (meaning there were no 'friendlies' in the area), and it gave them ample opportunity to test the new machine's mettle.

Early in November 1967 Anderson was assigned to 1st Aviation Brigade Headquarters, and his place was taken by Maj Richard Jarrett—a confirmed Cobra fan, who was with Seneff when the very first tentative ideas from Bell were put before Gen Westmoreland.

Dick has remained a staunch advocate of the aircraft, and joined Bell after his Army service. His main area of responsibility is the Middle East and Africa, and he never misses an opportunity to extol the virtues of the Cobra. In January 1968, however, he and his men were about to experience the Cobra's real baptism of fire—the Tet Offensive.

Tet

Timed to coincide with the lunar New Year celebrations (and therefore, typically for the North Vietnamese, a negotiated truce and ceasefire), the Tet Offensive was planned as a full-scale assault on the South, involving some 80,000 North Vietnamese Army (NVA) and Vietcong troops. Their targets were to include 36 out of 44 provincial capitals, five out of six autonomous cities, 23 airfields and military installations, plus numerous district capitals and hamlets. The objective was to catch the civilian and

The flamboyant Playboys *of 334th Armed Helicopter Company were in the thick of the fighting during the Tet Offensive. Their custom-made black flying suits reflected a certain 'style' that was always associated with the élite nature of Cobra units in Vietnam* (Bell)

LEFT
The Playboys' *patch maintained the stylish image — even though the word 'helicopter' was evidently spelt incorrectly in the original weave, as evidenced by the inked-in letter 'i'* (Bell)

military administrations off balance, with more than half their number on leave, and thousands of people moving around the countryside visiting relatives. It was also intended that the civil population join the National Liberation Front (NLF) and complete the destruction of the South's military capability.

Good intelligence and the premature launch of attacks in one area, gave the Allied forces some chance to prepare. Nevertheless, in the early hours of 31 January, the full fury of the invasion fell on military units who were, in many cases, under strength and unable to call up support. Significant attacks developed at Saigon, Hue, Quang Tri City, Da Nang, Dui Nhon, Kontum City, Ban Me Thuot, My Tho, Can Tho and Ben Tre.

The fighting was almost hand-to-hand, so TacAir and artillery units could not be called on to intervene. In most areas the only quick response was the helicopter gunship, and thankfully the UH-1 and Cobra were capable of great precision in these circumstances, often attacking enemy concentrations only the width of a narrow dirt road away from friendly troops—and frequently reversing the progress of an assault with their devastating firepower. Sometimes they were operating actually inside the perimeter of a base, receiving fuel and re-arming while hostile ordnance fell all around them. The turreted miniguns of the Cobra proved capable of almost surgical accuracy, bringing fire to bear not just on a building, but into the window the enemy was firing from.

Jarrett was woken by exploding rockets at 03.00 hr that morning, and immediately made his way to the Bien Hoa base area. He was quickly in the air over Saigon, but a 400 foot cloud base forced him and his wingman, Capt Jerry Childers, down low, and they came under fire almost immediately. Both aircraft were hit, and Childers was injured by shrapnel. With Jarrett acting as escort, the pair recovered safely to base. Jarrett and his Cobra were quickly back in the fight, joining the 'Playboys' of the 334th Armed Helicopter Company in strafing runs against VC positions near Long Binh.

Throughout this period many Bell civilian employees were with the Army in Vietnam, sharing the dangers and working like Trojans to keep the helicopters armed and flying. Turnarounds which should have taken 30 minutes were regularly completed, with engines running, in less than ten minutes—sometimes over very long duty periods of intense activity. When the main thrust of the attack was over, the Service officers were fulsome in their praise of this effort. 'The Army', wrote Jarrett at the time 'should have men like these.'

After many weeks of frantic activity the Tet Offensive faltered, and was finally stopped in its tracks. Slowly the South Vietnamese and US forces regained control. The civilian population never did rise in support of the North, despite the intimidation, torture and murder inflicted upon them by their communist 'liberators'. It had though, as the Duke of Wellington observed about an earlier campaign, been 'a damn close-run thing'. The undoubted turning point had been the introduction of the helicopter gunships. The new Cobra, operating in conditions of intense automatic fire, had shown that it was fully able to do what the Army asked of it.

In April 1968, only two years after ordering the first examples, the US Army ordered a further 98 aircraft, bringing the total up to 838.

Cavalry Heritage

During the late 1960s the Cobra began to reach operational units in growing numbers, and as tactics developed the aircraft continued to demonstrate its enormous potential. As an escort it provided really effective fire support all the way in and out of an LZ. Its crews sometimes flew 16 hour days during intensive operations, and the VC quickly discovered that it was the wrong type of helicopter to take a casual pot-shot at. One Cobra pilot recalls catching a .50 weapon pit with a two-second burst from the turret gun: 'Nothing left but hamburger and bits of scrap metal.'

The heritage of the airmobile force derives from old-style cavalry units, and the regulation drab aircraft colour scheme soon began to acquire appropriate embellishments such as crossed sabres and lance pennants, as well as the customary nose art so popular with American forces. In view of the Cobra's inviting profile, it came as no surprise when the first sharkmouth design appeared on the aircraft. Off-duty crews were highly conscious of their élite status, and could often be seen sporting black cavalry stetsons complete with crossed sabres and yellow cords.

It was the cavalry lineage that gave rise to the Cobra's most widely reported role, that of the killer element of the so-called 'pink team'. An airmobile cavalry troop typically consisted of three elements—the scouts were known as the 'white team', the guns were the 'red team', and the infantry (officially designated Aero-rifle Platoons, and known as 'grunts' in most other services) were 'blues'. When scouts flew with guns on a hunter-killer mission, the white/red combination was inevitably known as the 'pink team'.

Flying with the egg-shaped Hughes OH-6 Scout (an immensely popular and tough little machine, generally known as a 'Loach' from its original LOH-6 designation), the pink team Cobras were able to take the war to the enemy. Cobra pilots became adept at forward air control, often talking to air and ground units simultaneously, as well as handling their own weapons delivery in order to prevent the escape of an elusive adversary.

The reputation of the Cobra did not rest entirely on offensive operations. On 12 September 1968 Capt Ronald Fogleman, an F-100 Super Sabre pilot with the 3rd Tactical Fighter Wing, had his aircraft shot from under him while operating out of Bien Hoa. After a successful ejection, he parachuted into a rice paddy and was spotted by a flight of AH-1Gs. It seemed wise to move him immediately, and in the absence of spare seats in the Cobra he was carried some 20 miles to safety clinging to the external, downward-hinging weapons-bay door. Once this trick had been learned, many such rescues were carried out, and even 15 years after the Vietnam conflict virtually every USMC pilot operating over the Lebanon was seen with a decidedly unofficial snap-hook clipped to his harness. Clearly they too had decided that a draughty ride home was better than no ride at all, and the clip was an obvious safety precaution.

It was a constant source of concern to the Army aviators in Vietnam that the VC worked a lot at night. The Cobra was not originally built for night operations, and much effort was eventually expended on trying to provide it with an in-built night capability. In the interim, however, resourceful crews came up with a variety of 'lash-up' systems and tactics that worked remarkably well. One of the most successful was the development of 'Nighthawk' teams. For these operations a Cobra would provide the firepower, while a Huey, equipped with a starlight 'scope and a 50,000 watt searchlight, would provide the night vision 'eyes' and illumination. Often mounted in defence of base perimeters, these Nighthawk patrols were very effective. The enemy were generally unware of visual contact being established until the searchlight snapped on, and by that time it was far too late to avoid an almost instantaneous response from the Cobra.

No discussion about the helicopter war in SE Asia would be complete without touching on the vexed question of combat attrition. Much has been made of the apparently high losses suffered by American helicopters during the conflict, and as with any war situation claims and counter-claims are difficult to verify. A number of factors do have to be borne in the mind: first, the huge numbers of helicopters

actually deployed virtually guaranteed that the numerical losses would appear high; and second, the common idea that the Vietcong was a simple, peasant army is totally wrong, and seriously understates the quality of the opposition faced by the Americans. The VC was equipped with modern, sophisticated anti-aircraft weapons, and was more than capable of putting up a ferocious barrage of equally deadly small-arms fire.

A further difficulty in tracing actual combat losses results from the American tendency to rebuild almost total write-offs, which would then retain the original aircraft identity. This rebuilding operation was honed to a fine art, because the acquisition of spare parts was much easier to justify to a parsimonious Congress than requests for whole new aircraft.

Even allowing for these influences and for non-combat losses, the fact remains that nearly 800 Cobras (albeit mostly now modified to a higher standard) were still on the US Army inventory in 1987—this out of a total of nearly 1100 AH-1Gs delivered between 1967 and 1973. Considering that the aircraft was always operating at the sharp end of the battle, and that it was obviously a high-value target, the consensus opinion seems to be that the Cobra enjoyed a fairly high survival rate compared with other helicopters.

The Cobra's nose profile is an open invitation to the sharkmouth artist, and many variations have appeared during the aircraft's service. Note the twin landing lights in the extreme nose. These were later replaced by a belly-mounted retractable unit (Bell)

The XM-18 'Minigun' pod was a formidable anti-infantry weapon. The six-barrelled self-contained system held 1500 rounds of 7.62 mm ammunition, which could be fired at a devastating 4000 rounds per minute. Army Cobras are still able to carry the M-18, but the weapon is rarely seen these days (Mike Verier)

LEFT AND OVERLEAF
*Many hundreds of Cobras
were delivered to Vietnam,
the majority of them by sea.
This sequence of pictures,
taken in 1969, shows some of
the aircraft 'wrapped' for the
long journey, and then being
progressively assembled and
tested before flying off to their
combat units at the other end.
Some of the other deck cargo
includes CH-46 Sea Knight
helicopters, and OV-1
Mohawk and OV-10 Bronco
fixed-wing aircraft* (Bell)

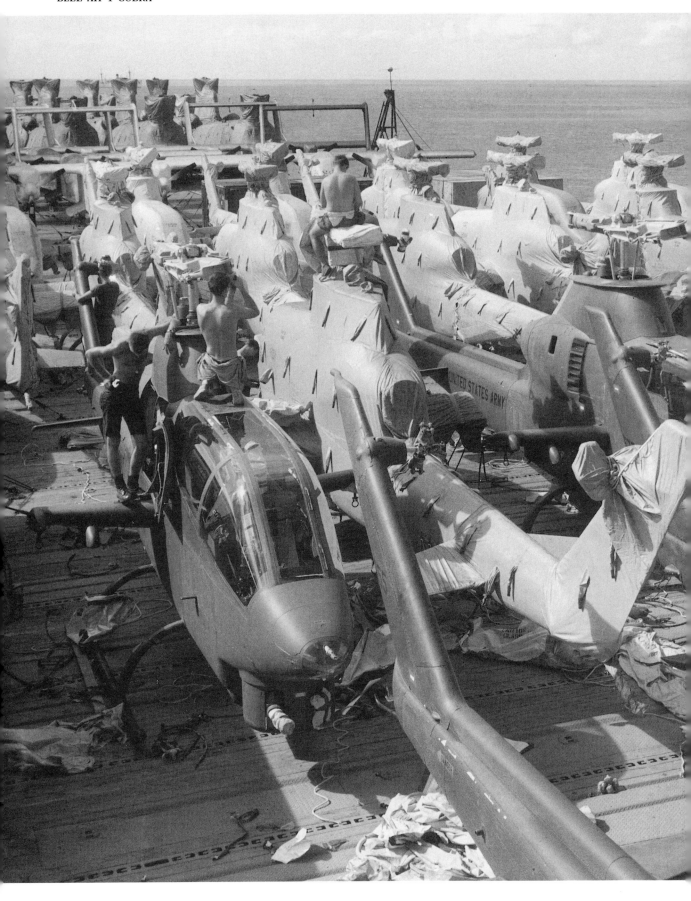

ABOVE
*Front and rear views of the awesome M-35 gun system.
This weapon was developed for the Cobra as the result of
pressure from Dick Jarrett's NETT unit in Vietnam, aided
by the drafting of a requirement under the series of
ENSURE programmes. Based on the 20 mm Vulcan rotary
cannon, the whole system weighed nearly 1200 lb, but it
gave the aircraft a considerable increase in effective range
and killing power* (Bell)

20 Millimeter Automatic Gun XM195. Gun XM195
is a six-barrel, rotary, electrically-driven, air-cooled
weapon that fires electrically-primed ammunition. It
is of the Gatling type, retaining a cluster of six barrels
in a rotor assembly which rotates within a stationary
housing. The rotor assembly contains tracks on which
six breech bolt assemblies, one for each barrel, slide
forward and back as the rotor assembly turns. The
forward motion of the breech bolt assemblies feeds
and chambers cartridges for firing. The backward
motion of the breech bolt assemblies extracts and
ejects the fired cases. The breech bolt assembly
motion is generated through interaction of breech
bolt guide rollers riding in a cam path machined into
the stationary rear housing assembly. Cartridges are
fired sequentially through each barrel at the same
position (approx. 12 o'clock) resulting in six cartridges
being fired per barrel cluster revolution. As each
breech bolt chambers a cartridge and rotates into
firing position, a drop-lock action secures it against
the firing reactive force. The dropping and lifting
actions necessary for bolt lock and unlock are
controlled by cam surfaces in the housing.

1. Electrical cable connector P295
2. Electrical cable connector P271
3. Electrical cable connector P272
4. Electrical cable connector P273
5. Electrical cable connector P274
6. Electrical cable connector P279
7. Electrical cable connector P280
8. Electrical cable connector P281
9. Gun drive assembly
10. Feeder gun feed chute assembly
11. Delinking feeder assembly XM87
12. Machine screw
13. Delinking ejection chute
14. Socket head cap screw
15. Hexagon head cap screw
16. Flat washer
17. Ejection chute assembly
18. 20mm automatic gun XM195
19. Gun mount assembly
20. LH lower forward panel assembly
21. RH lower forward panel assembly
22. LH lower aft panel assembly
23. RH lower aft panel assembly
24. RH chute support
25. LH chute support
26. Crossover gun feed chute assembly
27. Cross chute fairing installation
28. Wire rope assembly
29. LH ammunition box assembly
30. LH ammunition can-to-fuselage fairing assembly
34. LH forward fairing assembly
32. LH aft fairing assembly
33. Bellmouth assembly
34. Flexible chuting shield assembly
35. Booster switch assembly
36. LH rounds retainer
37. RH ammunition box assembly
38. RH ammunition can-to-fuselage fairing assembly
39. RH aft fairing assembly
40. RH forward fairing assembly
41. Ammunition booster assembly
42. Gun firing control unit
43. RH rounds retainer
44. RH wing attach adapter

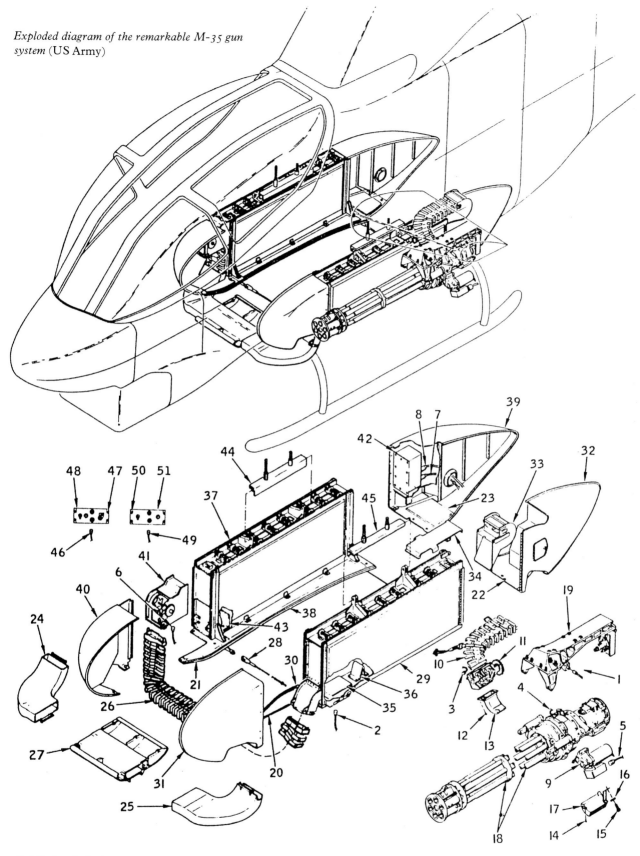

Exploded diagram of the remarkable M-35 gun system (US Army)

45. LH wing attach adapter
46. Electrical cable connector P282 (P/O aircraft wiring)
47. Turnlock fastener (P/O item 48)
48. Pilot armament control panel assembly

49. Electrical cable connector P286 (P/O aircraft wiring)
50. Turnlock fastener (P/O item 51)
51. Gunner armament control panel assembly

The M-35 system is instantly recognizable by the interlinked external ammunition sponsons at the top of the skid supports (Bell)

In-service developments

With any new and highly complex weapons system, the first field deployments quickly highlight the weaknesses and areas of necessary improvement. In the case of the Cobra these were comparatively few, probably because of its near-commonality with the Huey.

Early aircraft were delivered with tinted canopies in an effort to reduce the 'greenhouse effect' of the cabin. Both the tinting and the original ventilation system proved inadequate, as noted earlier, and a very efficient air-conditioning unit had to be installed. Other minor changes included the removal of the twin landing lights in the nose, and their replacement with a retractable lamp sited on the centreline immediately aft of the turret.

The decision to reposition the tail rotor was a far more significant modification. Moving it from the port side of the fuselage to starboard considerably reduced the masking effect of the tailfin, and cured the tendency of the aircraft to 'run out of left pedal'—a difficulty that was particularly noticeable when backing out of a revetment.

Cobras have also occasionally suffered from electrical problems—particularly the early machines, which had some inconsistencies in their wiring. The high humidity levels in SE Asia compounded the problem, as did weapons vibration and combat damage. One story that has passed into Cobra folklore illustrates this. It seems that a pilot hover-taxied to his take-off point quite normally, and turned his aircraft towards the tower in anticipation of seeing the green light. When it did not appear as expected, he keyed his transmit-mic in order to request clearance, and promptly fired two FFARs at the tower! The electrical gremlins were in fine form that day!

Armament development also proceeded with combat experience. The turreted minigun was highly effective, but it was always known that it lacked range and hitting power. The Cobra frequently carried M-18 pods on the wing stations, and although the extra guns added to the overall firepower, they were still only 7.62 mm weapons, which meant that they were tied to the same effective range limitations on the minigun. The M-18 was also an expensive piece of kit that was all too easy to jettison inadvertently.

The 2.75 inch FFARs were theoretically capable of longer range engagements, but their accuracy, even with scarfed nozzles to impart spin stability, was entirely dependent on how good the pilot was at allowing for 'Kentucky windage'. At least one crew discovered to their cost that rockets scrounged from the Air Force did not have the scarfed nozzles, and these were often more dangerous to the firer than to the intended recipient.

The answer to the range problem was generally seen as a larger calibre gun. The Cobra was going to have to wait some years for a fully developed M-197 turreted weapon, so the Army came up with the awesome (to the user) M-35 20 mm system. This six-barrelled revolver-type weapon was carried on the port inner pylon, with its 950 rounds of ammunition housed in two external boxes faired into aerodynamic sponsons above the skid supports. A cross-feed passed under the fuselage to link the forward ends of the two boxes, and flexible chuting finally led the rounds from the top rear of the port box to the gun. With ammunition, the whole system weighed 1187.4 pounds—three times the weight of an M-18 pod.

The M-35 gave the Cobra a powerful new punch which had a range in excess of 3000 m. It was not, however, without its problems. Such a big weapon produced vibration and muzzle-blast (overpressure) effects of such magnitude that the co-pilot had to be warned before firing commenced so that he could hold the canopy shut! Faced with so much vibration, the instruments and systems would sometimes give up and sulk for several minutes. Frequent popped rivets and other airframe blast damage eventually resulted in machines fitted with the M-35 having reinforced panels added to the port fuselage ahead of the wing.

Experimental programmes

The Cobra was involved in a number of experimental programmes during the late 1960s and early 1970s, many of which stemmed from the need to give the aircraft a night/adverse weather capability. Two of the most odd-looking were CONFICS and SMASH. These were both developed under ENSURE (Expedite Non-Standard Urgent Requirement for Equipment) programmes. Of the two, SMASH is perhaps the most familiar.

As acronyms go, the South-east Asia Multi-sensor Armament Sub-system for HueyCobra (SMASH) was rather contrived, but it had an effective ring to it. The programme resulted in an AH-1G equipped with an AN/AAQ-5 nose-mounted forward-looking infra-red (FLIR) sensor, then known as the Sighting Station—Passive Infra-red (SSPI). The aircraft also carried a podded AN/APQ-137 moving-target indicator radar, which was mounted on the starboard

This 'retired' AH-1G at Fort Rucker still carries the reinforced panels under the cockpit. These were designed to reduce the blast effects of the M-35 gun system (US Army via Mike Verier)

RIGHT AND OVERLEAF
The SMASH system seemed like a good idea at the time. It offered the crew a reasonably effective night-vision capability, but its weight and bulk reduced the range of the helicopter and severely curtailed the pilot's normal vision ahead of the display screen. These pictures show the fully equipped experimental Cobra, and some very early cardboard mock-ups of the proposed cockpit modifications (US Army, and Bell)

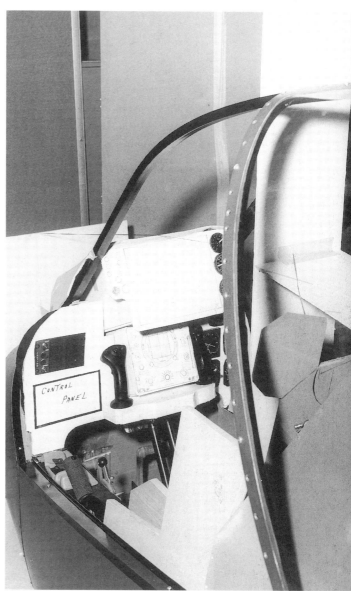

The CONFICS rig was designed to provide a night-vision capability by using low-light television (LLTV) sensors, but it too was unsuccessful, and the scheme was abandoned (US Army via Mike Verier)

ABOVE AND OVERLEAF
66-15248 shortly after delivery to Langley from the US Army's maintenance depot at Corpus Christie, and in its later NASA colour-scheme (NASA via Mike Verier)

outer weapons pylon. Display screens were available in both cockpits, and the system permitted the detection and engagement of both vehicular and personnel targets at night or in bad visibility. The FLIR also enhanced the pilot's ability to navigate in darkness. The aircraft retained the M-28 turret, and also carried the long-range M-35 20 mm gun and a seven-shot M-158 rocket launcher. The SMASH system was tested at Redstone Arsenal, but it failed to live up to expectations and was never deployed in Vietnam.

The Cobra Night Fire Control System (CONFICS) was a slightly simpler, if no less cumbersome, attempt to provide night vision capability by using low-light television. Developed under the ENSURE 100 programme, the Cobra system was derived from the Hughes Aircraft INFANT (Iroquois Night Fighter And Night Tracker) rig, which had earlier been mounted on UH-1M Hueys. It was originally intended that the system should control the Cobra's turret gun, and the sighting station was therefore built into the front cockpit. One aircraft (67-15761) was converted and underwent a period of testing at Redstone and Fort Rucker, but again the results were disappointing, and the Army went back to using flares and searchlights pending the arrival of more viable technology.

NASA's Cobra

One particular Cobra made a very significant contribution to aeronautical research. The third true production aircraft was 66-15248, and after a number of years in normal military service it was delivered from the US Army's maintenance depot at Corpus Christie, Texas, to NASA's Langley Research Center on 18 December 1972 for trials and test work.

Initially the aircraft retained its military drab colour, save for orange elevators, and the new designation 'NASA 541' applied to the tail boom above the 'United States Army' titling (both in white). Eventually however, in keeping with most NASA-operated types, the Cobra acquired a striking white paint scheme, with red and blue trim.

When the aircraft arrived at Langley it had a total of 515 airframe hours, and was fitted with an engine (serial LE 17603) that had run for only 446 hours. During its time with NASA it participated in a number of programmes concerning rotor aerodynamics and performance, as well as being involved in the investigation of acoustic phenomena. During the acoustic research the Cobra (then one of the Army's noisiest aircraft) could often be seen in formation with a Lockheed YO-3A 'Q-Star'—possibly the quietest powered aircraft in the world—which served as a mount for the microphones.

As noted earlier, the Cobra suffered some directional control and stability problems throughout its early service life, and wind-tunnel testing at Langley had led the aerodynamicists to suggest a 'butterfly' or V-tail as a possible solution. Bell had in fact received a contract to carry out preliminary design work, when a 1976 decision by NASA headquarters led to the relocation of all helicopter programmes to Ames Research Center, California, effectively cutting short all further work on the project.

Eventually, on 1 March 1978, the Cobra left Langley for its assignment to Ames, where its tail number was changed once more to 'NASA 736'. At the time of departure, it had accumulated 661.4 hours, still with the same engine.

Following several years at Ames as a chase aircraft, 66-15248 was returned to Army control in 1983, where it served with the California National Guard at Livermore. It was then delivered to the Bell plant at El Paso, Texas, for rebuilding as an AH-1S model. In early 1989, 15248 returned to Guard use fully reconditioned, and is, therefore, probably the oldest original Cobra airframe in service today. One cannot help wondering if pilots who fly the 'new' aircraft in years to come (many of whom will be younger than the airframe itself), will realize quite what an active life the old lady has had.

ABOVE LEFT
*Superimposed on the 'real' aircraft, this artistic impression
shows the strange tail arrangement proposed by NASA to
cure the directional stability problems. The badge under the
rear cockpit carries the legend 'US Army Air Mobility
R & D Laboratory'* (Bell via Mike Verier)

*During later test programmes at Ames, the tail number was
changed to NASA 736, i.e., the 7 denotes that facility*
(NASA via Bryan Wilburn)

Chapter 4
Metamorphosis

The Cobra had been an undoubted success during the Vietnam conflict, but it was clear to everyone that some improvements would be necessary if the machine was to remain effective in a more conventional scenario.

Many of the requirements had become obvious during combat, particularly the need for a larger calibre turret gun. This was originally recommended by the NETT unit, but the Army held back because the 2.75 inch rockets were consistently being fired with great accuracy during early operations. The Washington staff were misled by the fact that most of the NETT personnel were élite gunnery instructors, who could put rockets into the proverbial pickle barrel if necessary: this was certainly not true of the average pilot, and it took some years to realize the mistake.

The aircraft also needed better sensors, both to increase the stand-off range and to provide a night/adverse weather capability. The SMASH and CONFICS trials had given an indication of what might be possible, but their overall lack of success simply demonstrated that sensor technology was limited in the late 1960s.

One major advance that the Cobra could benefit from was the second generation of anti-tank missile. The potential of the aircraft in an anti-armour (as opposed to infantry support) role had been recognized quite early on, and it was well understood that a properly equipped attack helicopter could come close to being a 'flying tank' in terms of firepower and manoeuvrability.

The earliest anti-tank missiles—notably the French SS-11 (or M-22 in US service)—had been widely used by ground forces and successfully adapted to helicopter operation, but the shortcomings of these simple weapons were brought into sharp focus when North Vietnamese tanks crossed the border into the South.

In April 1972 the NVA launched the Easter Offensive, which turned out to be a full-scale invasion. The Americans had already started withdrawing their ground troops by that time, and were ill equipped to deal with the rapidly rising number of tanks. The unfortunate South Vietnamese troops, on whom all the ground fighting had devolved, were completely lost in the situation and powerless to stop the advance without immediate help. The few remaining M-22 launchers were hastily fitted to a handful of Hueys (the Cobra was not equipped to fire them), and the helicopters went into action. The missiles did manage to destroy a T-54 and a PT-76, but considering the total of 115 combat firings the weapon could hardly be described as cost-effective.

The Cobras did their best to repel the attack with 2.75 inch rockets. A recently developed HEAT (High Explosive Anti-Tank) warhead gave the FFARs a theoretical capability of destroying armoured vehicles, but in practice a number of good hits were needed before some of the heavier tanks could be taken out. One received 56 rounds before finally conceding, and it was only too clear that Army pilots would not be allowed the luxury of so many unimpeded passes over a similar target in Europe.

Because of the urgency of the situation in Vietnam, two UH-1Bs from Redstone Arsenal had their dramatic chequered colour schemes replaced by camouflage, and were dispatched to the front complete with their experimental weapons fit. The aircraft had been conducting trials with the Hughes TOW (Tube-launched Optically-tracked Wire-guided) anti-armour missile—a weapon that has

This early US Army AH-1G fires a salvo of 2.75 inch FFARs from the hover. The efflux flame has already disappeared from the first two rounds, although they are still less than 50 feet from the aircraft. Compare this with the awesome 5 inch Zuni rocket shown on pages 108–9 (Bell)

influenced Cobra development up to the present day.

TOW's introduction to the battlefield signalled the advent of a missile with genuine single-shot kill capabilities. Arriving on 24 April 1972, the mixed military and civilian personnel of the Helicopter Anti Tank Platoon (Provisional) were quickly deployed to the central highlands region in an effort to stem the NVA advance towards Kontum. Just over a week later the first enemy tank (an M-41) was destroyed, and in the course of 81 firings over the following two months the two modified Hueys accounted for no less than 26 tanks, and 33 other targets ranging from bunkers to barges. Clearly the new missile was a winner.

TOW was initially a tripod-mounted infantry weapon, with each round transported in a sealed cylindrical container which doubled as a firing tube when the whole assembly was clipped into the launcher. Vehicular mounting was no problem providing the vehicle was stationary during the engagement, and adaption for helicopter launch was the next logical step. With a range in excess of 3000 m, the weapon had the potential to keep relatively fragile helicopters at a safe stand-off distance from any target. The M-65 sighting system had sufficient magnification and stability to ensure the accuracy of rounds fired, and the fact that the missile was capable of destroying 'hard' targets such as reinforced bunkers was an obvious bonus. TOW had been specified for the AAFSS programme, and was under development for the AH-56 Cheyenne. Distinctive triple mounts with rather bulky (and eventually unnecessary) elevating aerodynamic fairings had been devised, and it was these that were adapted for the two UH-1s deployed to Vietnam.

Bell was aware that the AH-56 programme was already behind schedule, and becoming the subject of much inter-service rivalry. (The Air Force in particular failed to see why the Army needed a highly sophisticated, deep interdiction type, when that specific mission was regarded as their arena.) The

company management reasoned that if the Cobra fleet could be adequately upgraded, the package might well be sold to a cost-conscious Congress as an alternative to the ailing Cheyenne.

A private venture prototype had clearly paid dividends at the start of the Cobra programme, and now Bell, working in conjunction with its primary sub-system suppliers, could see the possibility of winning another big prize. The group of companies agreed to finance the construction of two prototypes to demonstrate their ideas. The aircraft would be loosely based on the single-engined AH-1G and twin-engined AH-1J airframes, but would incorporate all the improvements necessary to provide better performance and full systems integration. As they differed only in powerplant, both aircraft were to share the Bell designation Model 309 and the name KingCobra— carefully selected to maintain the snake connection while underlining the superiority of the new design. In September 1971, just nine months after the project go-ahead was agreed, the twin-engined aircraft made its first flight, followed by the single-engined 'Army' version in January 1972.

The KingCobra was certainly an impressive machine in terms of capability, and it had many features that Army aviators were not to see in the field until over a decade later. The fact that it failed to reach production is not so much a reflection of the machine itself, but rather a measure of the inability of the American procurement system at that time to arrive at a firm requirement for future equipment. The US political climate in the early 1970s was suffering from a crippling degree of anti-military backlash, following the ignominious withdrawal from Vietnam. Although the helicopter as a whole was not wanted, nearly all the features validated during the test programme found their way onto service Cobras at some stage. In fact, all of the developments beyond the AH-1G/J models have a direct link back to the KingCobra.

The Army test-flew the single-engined aircraft for some two and a half months during the summer of 1972. Nearly 60 hours were flown by four evaluation pilots at Alamosa, Colorado, and at the Fort Worth, Texas, flight-test facility, and all the design goals were verified. During the test period the aircraft was evaluated against the AH-56 and Sikorsky's new S-67 Blackhawk (not to be confused with today's S-70 (UH-60) Black Hawk transport helicopter).

The AAFSS concept was all but dead at that time. The AH-56 had won the original competition purely as a 'paper' aeroplane, but the real thing suffered major technical problems and cost escalations, all of which had the effect of putting it back onto the R & D budget in May 1969: this decision was instrumental in triggering both the S-67 and KingCobra programmes. The Army was also having second thoughts about the need for AAFSS and was now unsure about the type of aircraft it really wanted. The cost would certainly be a key consideration in the selection of any new programme.

ABOVE LEFT
The first TOW missiles in Vietnam were carried by two hastily deployed UH-1Bs from Redstone Arsenal. The experimental weapons fit included these bulky, semi-trainable launchers, which were later found to be quite unnecessary. The telescopic sight unit (TSU) is mounted on the lower port side of the aircraft, and the pilot's (starboard) windscreen includes a rudimentary aiming square. Just visible near the open door is a combat 'scorecard' showing the destruction of at least 18 tanks, two lorries, four jeep-type vehicles, and four smaller targets that are difficult to interpret (Museum of Army Flying via Mike Verier)

LEFT
The final service versions of the TOW launcher are remarkably unfussy pieces of kit. Without any aerodynamic finesse, they simply act as holders for the weapon's own transporter/launcher tube (Mike Verier)

It is always difficult to compare the costs of defence-related equipment, but in 1972 an AH-56 was reckoned at about $2.5 million 'fly-away', and $4.5 million fully equipped; whereas Bell had quoted a fully-equipped KingCobra at about $2.5 million. Another illustration of the difference was published in *Armed Forces Journal* for October 1971. The article pointed out that the AAFSS programme had cost some $200 million in Army R & D funds; had resulted in ten prototypes and a great deal of (admittedly useful) data, but still no operational system. On the other hand, having spent only about half as much again over the same period, the Army had acquired more than 900 operational AH-1G Cobras.

The confusion of choice facing the Army did not end purely with cost. The AH-56 was a deep penetration, day/night capable attack helicopter. KingCobra was also a dedicated attack aircraft with day/night capability, but its role was seen as anti-armour/infantry support at or near the forward edge of the battle area (FEBA). Sikorsky had adopted a different approach altogether. Their submission was a huge multi-mission machine, with a rotor diameter of 62 feet compared to the KingCobra's 48 foot disc. Based on the S-61 series, the Blackhawk had attack capability and an internal cabin for troops with a lower bay for fuel and ammunition, accessed from a hatch in the bottom of the fuselage, which could double as a rescue cabin.

Blackhawk, like the Russian *Hind* series developed

ABOVE
The Model 309 KingCobra flew for the first time in September 1971. The new prototype had full day/night avionics, and was the forerunner of most of the systems improvements incorporated into later Cobra variants. The aircraft is seen here fitted with a mock-up of the 13 foot span 'big wing' proposal. In the event, as noted in Chapter 7, the new wing was not pursued (Bell)

RIGHT
The Sikorsky S-67 Blackhawk attack helicopter was funded privately to compete with the KingCobra as a replacement for AAFSS. Based on S-61 dynamics, the Blackhawk was fully manoeuvrable, and capable of completing barrel-rolls (as seen here). Sadly, this very manoeuvre led to the demise of the one-off prototype, when the aircraft failed to recover from a roll and crashed—killing both pilots—at the 1974 Farnborough Air Display. The accident was later attributed to crew misjudgement (Sikorsky via Aldo Zanfi)

at about the same time, to which it bore a remarkable resemblance, had stub wings to provide extra lift.

The Army finally gave up on the AAFSS programme on 9 August 1972, when Acting Army Secretary, Kenneth E Beaulieu, announced that further funding had been stopped. Two days earlier, a final report from an evaluation task force headed by Maj Gen Sidney Marks, had concluded that none of the three aircraft on offer would meet the new Army requirement. The Cheyenne was larger and more complex than now required, the Blackhawk was too big, and the KingCobra too small—and all three aircraft were considered to be underpowered. After the cancellation of AAFSS a new requirement was drawn up for the Advanced Attack Helicopter (AAH), and the Army went back to Congress seeking funds for the project from FY 1973 onwards. Bell design staff then directed their attention towards the AAH programme and eventually submitted the Bell Model 409, which was selected as a finalist in the competition, and flew in October 1975 as the YAH-63.

Although the KingCobra had been formally rejected, the programme was not quite dead. The Army had taken note of the success achieved by TOW missiles in Vietnam, and did not want to wait for the weapon until AAH was available. Instructions were therefore given to start the integration of TOW into the Cobra fleet. The work was greatly eased by validation of the weapon and its systems on the KingCobra, and this effort eventually led to the range of general improvements incorporated into today's AH-1S(F) variant of the Cobra. The KingCobra was used for development work until 1974. The twin-engined aircraft crashed during this period, but the 'Army' version (now in a somewhat incomplete condition) was retired to the Army Aviation Museum at Fort Rucker. The contribution of these one-off prototypes to overall Cobra development was immense, and is explored in detail in Chapter 7.

AH-1S

The final trials to integrate the TOW system fully were carried out in 1973 under the Improved Cobra Armament Program (ICAP). This involved the modification of eight aircraft to carry the missile launchers, their associated M-65 sighting system, and the telescopic sight unit (TSU) in a nose-mounted optics turret. Also fitted at last was the Sperry-Univac helmet-mounted sighting system (HSS). First mooted when the prototype Cobra was flown, the developed HSS utilized a mechanical linkage that measured movement of the operator's head relative to the airframe. Operable by either crewman (whose helmets now incorporated a monocle sight), it meant that the turret gun was slaved to the operator's eyeline, and would continuously point wherever he was looking. This brought valuable savings in the time it

LEFT
An Army Cobra helmet complete with monocle sight. The aircraft attachment point for the HSS is just visible on top of the helmet, and the night-vision goggle fixings are seen on either side of the brow. Compare this high-tech piece of equipment with the simple 'bikers' style hard hat shown on page 15 (Mike Verier)

BELOW
The sole YAH-1R (70-15936), was basically an AH-1G Cobra modified to meet the standards of the ICAM programme. The aircraft retained its overall Olive-drab colour, but its 'Test' status required dayglo panels on the leading edge of the transmission 'dog-house' and on both sides of the nose. The black and white circles are purely for photographic reference (Bell)

RIGHT
An early AH-1S, showing the original canopy shape and the M-28 turret. The Playboys' *insignia is just visible on the transmission 'dog-house'* (Mike Verier)

took to respond to a threat, and after some practice, crews found that the system was remarkably accurate. The HSS could also be used to direct the TSU turret, which again clipped precious seconds off target acquisition time. The eight TOW-modified aircraft were designated YAH-1Q, and after completion of the qualification trials in 1974, Bell received an order to convert 92 AH-1G airframes to AH-1Q standard.

The AH-1Q was only intended as an interim configuration, because the weight of all the modifications meant that the aircraft was seriously underpowered. At the time, the Army was still examining its options. It was heavily involved in the AAH contest (which would ultimately lead to the AH-64 Apache), but it was clearly going to be some years before that

particular aircraft reached units in the field. After canvassing the various interested parties, a Recommended Operational Capability (ROC) paper was issued by the Department of Army Staff in December 1975, suggesting that the best way to update the attack helicopter force—at least until the arrival of AAH— was a far-reaching Cobra modification programme. This could be accomplished over a number of phases, and would not only incorporate all the improvements needed by the Army, but would also be extremely cost-effective because new airframes would not be needed.

The first phase had already been completed with the introduction of the AH-1Q. The next step was to increase the power margins, and again things were

already in hand. Uprated dynamics and more powerful engines were being applied to the basic airframe as part of the Improved Cobra Agility and Maneuvrability (ICAM) programme. Two aircraft were used in the qualification trials: an AH-1G (70-15936) which was redesignated YAH-1R, and an AH-1Q (70-16019) which became the YAH-1S. The modifications were fairly straightforward, involving the marriage of the 1800 shp Lycoming T53-L-703 engine to the already proven drive train employed on the KingCobra and the AH-1J 'International'—itself derived from the transmission used on the heavylift Huey Tug. The new engine and drive train successfully restored the performance margins eroded by the ever-increasing weight of the aircraft, and the combination was adopted as a full-scale modification to encompass all AH-1Qs and 198 AH-1Gs—290 aircraft in all. The common standard thus achieved was known as the 'Improved S'.

Meanwhile, the Army and the manufacturer had evolved a range of new features that would ideally be included in the 'ultimate' aircraft. It was intended to incorporate them in both new-build airframes on the production line, and, by progressive modification, into the remainder of the inventory so that all the helicopters would eventually be brought up to the same standard. The next step therefore, would be the 'Production S'—100 of which were manufactured with all the ICAM/ICAP improvements noted above, and a completely redesigned cockpit surrounded by distinctive 'flat plate' canopies to reduce the glinting problem during combat. These machines were also fitted with 10kVA alternator, the bulged housing for which provided a recognition feature for these and all subsequent models. The penultimate step in what was to become the definitive 'S' model Cobra saw the adoption of the M-197 3-barrelled, revolver-type cannon, mounted in the so-called 'universal' turret.

Sometimes referred to as 'Upgun' Cobras, 98 of these were built under the Enhanced Cobra Armament System (ECAS) programme.

The final stage in the transformation of the Cobra came with the machine originally known as the 'Modernized S'. Characterized externally by the ungainly bulk of its exhaust suppression equipment, this variant finally brought together all the improvements of ICAP, ICAM and ECAS, and a number of its own changes. As the current production model for both the US Army and export customers, the introduction of further improvements is an ongoing process and production totals continue to rise. At the time of writing, well over 100 airframes have been manufactured to this standard, and the process of running the various earlier models through the modification programme is nearly complete. At the extreme, AH-1G airframes are stripped to the bare framework at Bell's Amarillo facility, and completely rebuilt.

All this effort has resulted in an aircraft that will remain in front-line service for many years. In the process it has changed little in overall shape, but its weapons capability has vastly improved to enable it to remain effective over the battlefields of the 1990s. To understand how this has been achieved it is necessary to look in some detail at the various systems that go together to make up what until 1988 was referred to as the AH-1S(MC).

Improvement Analysis

In order to remain effective on any modern battlefield, a weapons system must be capable of surviving in an intensely hostile environment, delivering its ordnance load accurately, and returning safely to fight again. By the end of the 1960s the AH-1G Cobra was starting to fall short of these ideals—a situation that could cause particular concern in the technologically sophisticated European theatre. The Cobra had already been on the receiving end of advanced anti-aircraft weaponry, when the Soviet SA-7 *Strella* surface-to-air missile was encountered in SE Asia. This relatively simple infantry weapon was easily carried and operated by one man, but it was more than capable of hacking down a helicopter. The hastily installed partial counter to this threat was a shroud to redirect the exhaust plume up into the rotor. This made it much more difficult for the missile's seeker head, but the modification had an adverse effect on the helicopter's performance, and was at best only an interim measure. In Europe the aircraft would face the highly effective, radar-guided ZSU-23 anti-aircraft (triple-A) system, and missiles that were far more advanced than the SA-7, so the designers of the AH-1S had a formidable problem to cope with—quite apart from fully integrating the TOW system.

The first step in the quest for survivability was to minimize the 'signature' of the aircraft, not only in the

LEFT
*The standard AH-1S production aircraft has a 'flat plate'
cockpit canopy. Note also the bulged housing for the 10kVA
alternator, which can be seen close to the intake* (Michel C
Klaver)

BELOW LEFT
*The upturned 'sugar scoop' exhaust directs the hot gases into
the rotor. This diffusion makes it more difficult to lock on
with an IR-seeking missile, but it also carries performance
penalties* (Museum of Army Flying via Mike Verier)

RIGHT
*The new IR-countermeasures include a heat-absorbent paint
finish, the Garrett suppressor to cool the exhaust, and the
AN/ALQ-144 active IR-jammer which swamps the
incoming seeker with confusing returns* (Mike Verier)

infra-red and radar regions, but also acoustically and
visually (the old maxim that you can't shoot what you
can't see is as true as ever in the electronic age).
Because a helicopter can fly very low, and change its
direction rapidly, it can always give radar-guided or
ballistic weapons a hard time in trying to reach a firing
solution, but an infra-red (IR) missile, once locked
on, is very difficult to shake off. Attention was
therefore first directed towards the IR part of the
problem, both to reduce the chances of a lock, and
then to confuse the missile's seeker if the lock was
achieved. Three lines of defence were used, two
passive and one active. The primary passive measure
was a new exhaust suppressor produced by Garrett
Air Research. This unit consists of a cooled-plug type
suppressor in the engine exhaust stream, itself
surrounded by a shroud designed to introduce more
ambient air into the exhaust plume. The system is
very effective, and it significantly reduces the range at
which IR weapons can achieve a lock, for a total
weight of only 65 lb and a claimed performance
penalty of less than 2.5 per cent. The second layer of
passive defence was the adoption of a totally matt,
dark green paint finish, which apart from its obvious
visual camouflage qualities, is heat absorbant and
therefore helpful at the IR end of the spectrum. The
effectiveness of the finish can be attested to by anyone
who has tried to photograph the Cobra. Light seems
to fall into the colour and frequently results in a
picture of what appears to be nothing more than a dark
shape! Despite these passive precautions, there will be
occasions when either the range or sensitivity of a
seeker allows a lock to be achieved. To deal with these
cases an AN/ALQ-144 active IR jammer produced by
Sanders Associates is used. The unit is actually an
electrically heated ceramic IR source (requiring no
less than 54 amps in operation) designed to swamp an
incoming seeker with confusing returns. The exact
efficiency of the 28 lb 'disco lights' system—which can
be seen mounted above the engine exhaust—is of
course classified, but its adoption by virtually the
entire US Army and Marine helicopter force may be
taken as an indication of satisfied customers.

Europe-based Cobras will have to operate in an
extremely difficult electronic environment, which
necessitates the inclusion of on-board detection and
electronic countermeasures (ECM) equipment if the
aircraft are to survive for long. Use was therefore
made during the update of an AN/APR-39 radar
warning receiver (RWR). A cockpit display gives the
pilot the direction of the threat and its range, and a
simultaneous audio tone tells him what sort of threat
he faces (the pulse-doppler gun-laying radar of a
ZSU-23, for example, has a very distinctive tone).

Because the range of tones that a pilot needs to memorize is becoming confusing, the AN/APR-39 will gradually be replaced by the more capable AN/APR-59, which is already in service with the US Air Force. The new receiver will give more information on the cockpit display, and the signal analysis will be handled by the system computer. Similar equipment to warn of laser illumination has been tested, but not yet operationally deployed. The Cobra's active ECM defence currently consists of the AN/ALQ-44 radar jammer, which can disrupt most gun-laying radars now in use. It should also be borne in mind that the Cobra's new rotor blades are made of composite materials, giving a significant reduction in the overall radar signature of the aircraft—although this was not the primary reason for their selection.

With the widespread adoption of nap-of-the-earth (NOE) flying techniques, accurate tactical navigation assumed an even greater importance than hitherto. While full use is still made of conventional maps (and even Kit Carson-style tracking on occasions) matters are greatly assisted by the AN/ASN-128 lightweight doppler system. This very compact unit weighs only 28 lb, and has a cockpit display with present position indicator (PPI) facility, which provides course, speed and distance read-outs to any one of six preselected locations. Positioning is accurate to two per cent of distance travelled, and the system can be updated in flight. It can also be used to update the range to target display when used in conjunction with the laser rangefinder and fire-control computer. The aircraft is also being equipped with the AN/ARN-123 CONUS (Continental US) navigation system, which will open up the long range capabilities of the overall system.

One of the most important areas of development in the combat helicopter field over recent years, has been the precision with which a successful 'first-shot' attack can be made. The integrated fire-control system on the current Cobra is probably one of the most accurate ever flown operationally. The heart of the system is a computer which combines inputs from a number of sub-systems to give previously unattainable weapon accuracy, at last freeing the crew from having to allow for 'Kentucky windage' when firing guns and rockets. The main difficulty with helicopter armament has always been the impossibility of assessing the aircraft's true motion using conventional pitot-static sensors. Even with the aircraft at the hover, rotor downwash negates any attempt to determine ambient wind speed and direction. A significant Cobra 'first' was the adoption of the British-developed Air Data System (XM-143 in US service) from Marconi Avionics. Mounted on a distinctive boom protruding from the starboard side of the cockpit, this system provides for the first time, accurate, high-quality air data which combines with information from the laser rangefinder and doppler navigation system to produce firing solutions for ballistic weapons. The accuracy thus attained is well within the Army's required CEP (circular error probable), giving new life to the trusty 2.75 inch FFARs, and greatly increasing the chance of a first hit with the 20 mm cannon. More interesting still is the capability the system gives the pilot in the self-defence air-to-air gunnery role! Linked into the system are the TSU, the pilot's head-up display (HUD), and the rocket management panel.

Flying NOE in an environment that is hostile in every sense of the word is very demanding on the pilot, and the HUD, developed by the Kaiser Company, displays all the important information he needs, on a clear glass screen mounted above his instrument panel. The display is focused on infinity, so he can fly the aircraft without having to look down into the cockpit or constantly refocus his eyes. The information available includes basic flight parameters—attitude, height, speed, heading and engine torque—together with range to target, and rectangles that define the limitations of manoeuvre imposed by the wire-guided TOW missile.

The pilot's workload is further eased by an improved and far more sensitive stability and control augmentation system (SCAS), which, for instance, will happily compensate for the considerable recoil effect of the 20 mm gun—especially when firing to either side of the centreline. One other significant addition to the pilot's cockpit is a new management panel for the wing stores, which bestows great flexibility on the 2.75 inch rockets. Using this panel, a mixed load can be carried and fired selectively. The load can consist of rockets with a variety of high explosive (HE) warheads and either impact or proximity fuses, rockets carrying sub-munitions, and warheads of smoke or white phosphorous (WP, or 'Willy Pete' to the crews) for target marking. The panel will show the number of rounds remaining by type, and enable the selection of whatever launch mode—single, pairs, multiple pairs, etc—or fuse setting the pilot might require. Range to target can either be entered manually or taken from the laser rangefinder, and the fire control computer will update the information during an attack. As a result, accurate indirect fire is now possible out to a range of some 6000 m.

The formerly austere gunner's 'office' has also acquired a number of additional instruments and systems. Prominent in the centre of the panel is the large 'scope' of the TSU. This is linked directly to the optics turret mounted in the extreme nose of the aircraft, and provides precision tracking for the TOW rounds. The optics system offers a choice of wide-angle ×2 magnification for rapid initial target acquisition, or a ×13 narrow field for identification and tracking. The coverage of the sight extends to 110

The XM-143 Air Data System has its primary sensor mounted on a distinctive boom extending from the starboard side of the cockpit (Mike Verier)

degrees in azimuth, and from + 30 degrees to − 60 degrees in elevation. The optics turret also contains the laser rangefinder, and the whole assembly can be directed onto a target by the gunner's hand control, or by the helmet sight (HSS) of either crewmember. The turret has provision for the future inclusion of a forward-looking infra-red (FLIR) system, which would help to give the Cobra night/adverse weather capability. At the time of writing, funding has only just been agreed for the FLIR system, and not yet for the proposed AN/AAS-32 laser tracker. The tracker is designed to search for and acquire laser designated targets (designation can be from remote ground or airborne sources, or conceivably from an on-board designator). Once a lock has been achieved, the system will slew the TOW sight onto the target. It seems likely that this system will be fitted if the US Army ever decides to re-arm the Cobra fleet with the AGM-114A Hellfire, or similar laser-guided munitions.

All this new equipment adds considerably to the technical complexity of the aircraft, and the complete fire-control system has a self-test facility (BITE, or built-in test equipment) which enables everything to be checked automatically on start-up. Should a fault show up, the components of the system can be quickly checked (they all have a 'go/no go' indicator) and replaced if necessary. The use of line-replaceable units allows the repair of modules to be completed in

the workshops without any need to ground the aircraft.

Having discussed the primary (TOW) and secondary (FFAR) armament, this would seem a good point to look at the turret gun. The trainable gun has been a highly successful feature of the Cobra since its inception, but it has not been universally adopted by subsequent attack helicopter designers—so why is it retained on the AH-1S? Basically because experience in combat has emphatically validated the concept: the gun remains a flexible and comparatively cheap weapon, which is effective in a wide range of situations. Although the original rifle-calibre weapon in the M-28 turret produced devastating results against infantry or 'soft' targets, the advent of man-portable surface-to-air missiles (SAMs), and some of the larger calibre radar-guided triple-A, simply proved that the gun did not have sufficient 'reach' to keep the helicopter itself out of trouble. The result was the 'universal' turret, currently mounting a 20 mm M-197 triple-barrelled gun, but also capable of accepting 25 mm and 30 mm alternatives. The M-197 system has the capacity for 750 rounds of ammunition, which provides a total firing time of about 60 seconds, and active fire control gives the gun a remarkable accuracy (again, well within the Army's required CEP) out to some 2000 m or more. The weapon is highly thought of by Cobra crews because it provides a valuable suppressive capability during the

vulnerable moments of TOW launch and guidance. This period can be as long as 30 seconds at maximum missile range, during which the helicopter's freedom of manoeuvre is severely constrained by the need to keep within the TOW's post-launch envelope. Using the wide field of fire offered by the turret, the pilot can aim the weapon with his helmet-mounted sight, and apply suppressive fire while the gunner concentrates on tracking the TOW.

At unit level an increase to 30 mm is seen as unnecessary. The extra range would be of marginal value, and the increase in weight would inevitably translate into fewer rounds of ammunition. The US Marine Corps has recently qualified the M-197 to fire the plastic-sheathed, depleted uranium rounds used by the US Navy's Phalanx shipboard air defence system. These have twice the velocity (and therefore half the gravity drop) of a conventional round, and at the receiving end they have three times the penetrating power. This means that the rounds are not only more accurate (because of their flatter trajectory), but they are also more effective on arrival. The USMC's motives for the change may include commonality with the Navy's ammunition stocks, but there can be no doubt that the increased effectiveness is an attractive option for the Army.

The remaining major changes that produce a modernized AH-1 S concern the canopy and the rotor. The Cobra's original fighter-type canopy was not only aesthetically very pleasing, but it also provided the crew with the best possible all-round visibility. Unfortunately its curved shape also gave off random reflections that could betray the aircraft's position at a considerable distance—especially when seen from above. To minimize this problem, a new canopy was evolved that cut out the curves and, coincidentally, gave slightly more headroom in what was becoming a very cramped cockpit. The opportunity was also taken to make it part of the escape system, inasmuch as small explosive charges can now blow off the two doors and cut the remaining side windows from the canopy structure, in the event of what the Americans term 'an emergency egress situation'. The new angular shape also reduces radar reflection (and, incidentally, gave rise to the 'flat plate' appellation, despite actually having bulged side panels). All this has been achieved at the expense of some visibility and speed, but the US Army—unlike the Marine Corps—considers it worthwhile.

The AH-1 S has been fitted with new K-747 main rotor blades developed by Kaman Aerospace Corporation—itself no stranger to helicopter dynamics. Of composite construction, the new blade is distinguishable by its wider chord and tapered tips. It has the advantages of greatly improved battle tolerance (taking hits from 23 mm HE rounds without failure) and, because of its non-metallic structure, a much smaller radar signature. The aerofoil design reduces the characteristic 'truck' noise that always heralds the arrival of a Cobra ('lower acoustic detectability' in US defence-speak), and the strength of composite materials gives the K-747 a time between overhauls in excess of 10,000 hours—a tenfold increase on the figure set for metal blades. The blades are also said to be up to 75 per cent repairable at unit level, which is a significant advantage considering the number of tree and bird strikes that occur during European operations.

Fighting Ability

Some authorities have expressed doubts about the ability of any attack helicopter to survive on a modern battlefield, and with the arrival in service of the highly sophisticated AH-64 Apache, it would be tempting to assume that the 20-year-old Cobra design was now obsolescent, if not actually obsolete.

After discussing the situation with operational Cobra crews, it seems clear to this author that they have considerable confidence in the aircraft. They, more than anybody, appreciate the magnitude of the threats they face, and the limitations of the Cobra itself. Nonetheless they are still confident that the aircraft will deliver, and bring them through the battle. This is not a display of mere bravado, but an attitude of sensible professionalism. The challenge of flying the attack mission has traditionally attracted the best people, some transferring from other services and even giving up the chance of career enhancement in order to fly the Cobra. They are professional soldiers, prepared to live 'in the mud' with their aircraft, and are something of an élite in the helicopter community. 'After all,' they will ask you with a wry grin 'how many helicopter drivers get to fly *between* the trees, and be paid for it as well?'

The Cobra does, however, have its limitations. Its present role could hardly have been envisaged—or indeed catered for technically—at the time of its inception. Its most obvious drawback is the lack of true night/adverse weather capability. The aircraft can be *flown* at night now that the cockpit lighting has been adapted for night-vision goggles, but actually fighting at night or in poor visibility is another matter. It has been made clear in the past that the restriction on the necessary FLIR system is financial rather than technical, and budgetry priorities may change now that more reliance is being placed on conventional weapons in Europe.

A second major limitation is the rotor system. In common with all other designs of its generation, the Cobra cannot tolerate negative G conditions (in fact the lower end of the envelope is +0.5 G). This necessitates particular care in 'pop-up' manoeuvres for instance, but the problem is not too restrictive. The use of a two-bladed rotor also gives rise to the 10,000 lb gross weight limit of the AH-1S. This arbitary number has nothing to do with the transmission or available power, but is set by the autorotation capacity (i.e., the maximum weight the rotor will support in the event of engine failure). Consequently, any further increase in airframe or equipment weight will have to be traded off against armament or fuel, and any new piece of kit, no matter how desirable it may be, is greeted with the inevitable question by the crews: 'Yes, but how much does it weigh?'

In Europe the US Army AH-1s are divided into Cavalry and Attack units. The Cavalry Troops provide security and 'muscle' at the flanks of any NATO thrust, and are used to confuse and harass the enemy in the hope that he will divide and ultimately dilute his attack. The Attack units themselves form a highly mobile 'fire brigade' force, designed to make use of the attack helicopter's fundamental asset—the ability to move and concentrate firepower with great speed and flexibility. Each helicopter company has about 21 Cobras and 12 OH-58 Kiowa scouts, nominally divided into three equally equipped platoons of seven attack and four scout aircraft. To allow for scheduled maintenance and minor mishaps, the basic fighting strength of a platoon is set at five Cobras and three Kiowas, which in battle can further subdivide into 'light' (2 + 1) and 'heavy' (3 + 2) teams. Tactical control is held by a Battle Captain in another OH-58 or a Huey.

Given the NATO assumption that a build-up of political tension will provide some warning of an impending attack, the various elements will be dispersed to prearranged Forward Arming and Refuelling Points (FARPs). On being called in by the ground commander, the scout's job is to probe forward until the position and strength of the opposing formations can be established, and then direct the Cobras into the most appropriate firing positions. The tactics are constantly rehearsed, and the degree of co-ordination between the crews is very impressive. A pattern of hand and aircraft movement signals has been established to allow continued communication in conditions of radio silence or intense jamming, and these can be discerned over surprising distances by using the Cobra's TSU system. Working as they do from preassigned FARPs, the crews quickly build up a comprehensive knowledge of the topography of 'their' patch of the battlefield, and this familiarity with every tree, bush and hiding place in the area gives them a decisive edge over an enemy who will be approaching hostile territory with extreme caution.

During actual engagement, the tactic is to constantly keep firepower on the enemy, forcing him to operate in the restrictive visibility of a closed down vehicle. As one team unmasks and fires, the other is moving to a new location, so the direction of attack is constantly changing and unpredictable. Attacks can also be co-ordinated with artillery and other ground-based anti-tank weapons, and the Cobra has a useful indirect fire capability with its 2.75 inch FFARs against targets that are either beyond the range of the

The Wire Strike Protection System (WSPS) guides and cutters can be seen immediately above the pilot's head, and on the lower fuselage, just aft of the turret (Mike Verier)

TOW, or simply too 'hot' to get at without putting the helicopter at risk. Cobras can also be used to form part of a Joint Air Attack Team (JAAT), which is a co-ordinated set-piece assault by helicopters, US Air Force A-10s, and other NATO strike aircraft. Artillery and other ground-based assets can also be brought into the fray, but the whole thing needs time and considerable planning. For this kind of attack, the AH-1s can carry white phosphorous FFARs for accurate target marking.

In the European theatre of operations the Cobra's ability to fly NOE is exploited to the full, as are its small size and agility. NOE flying is obviously not without its hazards, and this has recently resulted in the addition of a Wire-Strike Protection System (WSPS)—an arrangement of wire cutters and guards around the front of the aircraft. These protect the crew and the rotor mast from the danger of collision with telephone wires and small power cables, but naturally offer only limited help if the helicopter tangles with a large grid line. The roof-mounted WSPS cutter has proved a real boon to the pilot on a hot day, because the mounting plate keeps the sun off the back of his neck!

Much has been made of the threat posed to the attack helicopter by various Warsaw Pact anti-aircraft systems. While there can be no denying that they all have lethal potential, most of the systems rely on predictable technology (radar, IR-seekers etc) to acquire and 'lock' their targets. Understanding how the lock works allows it to be broken, either by clever tactical flying or by using even more technology to jam or confuse the seeker. Despite the complex systems ranged against them, the threat the Cobra crews fear most is the man with an automatic rifle they haven't spotted: he is unpredictable, virtually impossible to detect with any of the on-board sensors, and likely to damage aircraft and crew if he gets the chance of a first-burst attack. The aircraft is particularly vulner-

able during NOE operations, which are often flown virtually at walking pace and only a few feet from the ground.

The Soviet-made ZSU-23 is used extensively throughout the WarPac alliance, and is probably one of the most effective cannon-based anti-aircraft systems in service anywhere in the world. Its pulsed doppler guidance system can lock on to a target in less than eight seconds, and its 23 mm HE rounds are lethal out to a range of some 3000 m. Having said that, the acquisition of a helicopter flying NOE is by no means certain, and the Cobra has a particularly small radar signature. The RWR can detect the incoming signals, classify them, and apply the appropriate jamming countermeasures. The gunner is then reduced to using the ZSU-23's optical system, but to do this he must first see the Cobra—no easy matter in the European environment. Add to this the fact that the tracked ZSU-23 is a relatively lightly-armoured vehicle, and it is easy to see why the Cobra is no pushover as a target. If the helicopter fires back, particularly with its FFARs which outrange the ZSU's cannon by a considerable margin, the vehicle itself becomes vulnerable—especially in the region of the external water-jackets that cool its guns.

The other ground-to-air threat that poses a significant problem to the Cobra is the IR-seeking missile—particularly the shoulder-launched weapon, which again has that element of unpredictability. Initial acquisition remains a fundamental problem to the missile operator, and the modernized aircraft has a number of provisions to make this even more difficult. The carriage of flare dispensers would be a possibility, but only at the expense of some armament or fuel, and the value of flares during NOE operations—when the helicopter is closest to the enemy and therefore in most danger—is questionable. The best defence is still to keep as low as possible, in the certain knowledge that any IR seeker will find it difficult to lock on to a target moving below and within the tree line.

The problem that has most occupied the Army's thoughts over recent years has been the prospect of specifically anti-helicopter operations by other

ABOVE
Close-up of the receiver antenna for the radar countermeasures set. Below it, on the forward-facing rim of the 'dog-house', is the spherical bulge that will house the laser scanner/tracker (Mike Verier)

TOP
Fifteen old AH-1Ss have been fitted with the PNVS part of the Apache system and are used at Rucker to train pilots to take off and land 'under the hood' without risking an expensive AH-64 (via Mike Verier)

ABOVE
Other than NASA, the only 'civilian' user of the Cobra has been the US Customs Service, who used its speed and manoeuvrability to pursue low-flying smugglers. Armament was restricted to the crew's personal weapons and the turret gun was replaced by a powerful 'Nitesun' searchlight (Brian Nicklas via Mike Verier)

helicopters. Until now it has not been part of the attack helicopter's job to 'mix it' on an air-to-air basis, the crew always relying on evasion tactics to avoid coming under attack from conventional aircraft. The development of later versions of the Mi-24 *Hind* has ended all that. Recognising the threat posed by NATO's attack helicopters, WarPac units are now being tasked specifically with their destruction. The *Hind* is bigger and faster than the AH-1, and it can carry more armament, including, presumably, IR missiles. Something it does lack is manoeuvrability, particularly at low speed and low altitude, and its crews have to operate it rather like a conventional aircraft, relying on first-pass firepower to make a kill. This means that it can be outflown by an alert Cobra crew. 'Survival', they will tell you 'is a matter of doing your job well and having your head where it ought to be.' Ultimately we may yet see the emergence of true 'fighter' helicopters, but in the meantime it would be a very unwise *Hind* pilot who overlooked the Cobra's agility, and its 20 mm counter-punch.

Drug busters

There have been two 'civil' users of the Cobra—albeit government agencies. The second of these has a small but distinguished niche in Cobra history, involving the AH-1S.

Between December 1981 and May 1986 the US Customs Service used Cobras for aerial interdiction of drug smugglers. The vast profits being made from illegal drugs have always allowed the smugglers to use fast, modern aircraft and boats to get them into the country. The Coast Guard and Customs Service have needed to turn increasingly to the military to find a means of combating these sophisticated criminals.

The Cobra came into the picture because its speed and agility enabled it outrun most of the general aviation types then being used. The helicopters were operated stripped of armament and armour, and the turret gun was replaced by a powerful searchlight. Because most of the illegal flights took place at night, operations would often be conducted by a FLIR-equipped USMC OV-10D. These aircraft could sit unseen some thousands of feet above an unsuspecting smuggler, who felt safe enough, flying totally blacked-out and well below any radar detection. The Cobra would be vectored onto the target aircraft via the secure speech channels available on military radios, and the startled pilot could often be induced to surrender on the spot when he was suddenly illuminated by a mean-looking black helicopter.

The major limitation of the Cobra in this kind of operation was its two-man crew. The pilot had to stay with the aircraft at least until shut-down, which meant that one man had to handle the arrest of an unknown number of very unwilling suspects. Leaving a Cobra unattended with its engine running is neither sensible, nor safe (it *has* been tried, and on at least one occasion an inadequately frictioned-down collective shook itself loose, and left the crew watching helplessly as the aircraft attempted to take off on its own—just before toppling over and beating itself to death). The Cobra was nevertheless able to contribute significantly to the war on drugs over a period of nearly five years. It was gradually replaced in the role from 1973 onwards by the UH-60 Black Hawk, which has a greater range and carrying capacity.

Chapter 5
Two into Four

One of the few perceived limitations of the Cobra is the teetering rotor. With good reason, Bell have kept faith with the two-blade system. Nevertheless, they have continued to work on the four-blade rotor as it offers trade-offs which would make it more suitable for certain mission profiles.

By using advanced design techniques and modern materials, it is possible to craft a multi-blade rotor system that is both lighter than its two-bladed counterpart, and capable of absorbing more power. This in turn means that the rotor has a greater G tolerance, which immediately opens up the flight envelope and increases the agility of the helicopter— an advantage that will always be welcomed by combat pilots. Four-bladed systems also tend to be less noisy, and their vibration levels are much lower.

The first experimental system designed by Bell flew on a civil Model 206L-M Long Ranger in 1978, and the subsequent testing and demonstration period accounted for more than 800 hours in the air. This was followed by a production system designed and certified for a variant of the Huey-derived Model 212. The four-bladed aircraft was redesignated Model 412, and the first of two 'prototypes' flew during August 1979. After certification, the first new-build examples of the 412 came off the production line in 1981, and at the same time retro-fit hub-and-blade kits were manufactured to enable existing 212 owners to convert their aircraft to the new 412 standard.

With all this work on multi-blade systems going on, the company engineers inevitably looked at the prospect of mating the 412 rotor with the Cobra airframe. Such a union would provide an increase in payload and performance that could broaden the appeal of the aircraft considerably: it was also a low-risk modification that would enable Bell to continue its policy of product improvement by evolution rather than revolution.

Accordingly, in December 1979, the Model 249

was flown. This aircraft was a modification of the YAH-1S prototype (70-16019), and with its four-bladed rotor it soon proved to be fast and responsive. Following the success of the trials, a number of proposals were made to the military based on the multi-blade Cobra, all of which were aimed at extending the useful battlefield life of the aircraft well into the 1990s.

The first of these was the 'improved attack' Cobra (sometimes referred to as the Cobra II in Bell publications). This was to feature a 2000 shp engine, multiplexed wiring, and a full IR-sensor/sighting-system in place of the standard 'optronics' package. The aircraft would therefore be compatible with both AGM-114A Hellfire and TOW missiles, possess a realistic night/adverse weather capability, and perform better during NOE flight. The company suggested that the required modifications could all be incorporated during the remanufacturing cycle of the original 290 'Modernized S' aircraft. In the event, the Army rejected the proposal virtually out of hand, and put big money into the even more advanced Light Helicopter Experimental (LHX) programme instead. Presumably the faintest whiff of interest in the Bell proposals would have prompted someone in Congress to ask why the very expensive LHX was needed at all,

ABOVE RIGHT
This commercial derivative of the twin-engined Huey, the Bell Model 412, provided the rotor technology that was used on the four-bladed Model 249 Cobra (Bell)

RIGHT
Sporting its optional 'unarmed' nose, the experimental Model 249 was the first Cobra to fly with a four-bladed main rotor. Aerodynamic changes were also made to the 'surfboard' fairing at the top of the transmission pylon (Bell)

LEFT
The Model 249 in its 'Cobra II' guise. Note the extended-chord tailplane, with what appear to be slots or tiny elevator-type devices along the trailing edge. This configuration could have been achieved with a straightforward retro-fit programme (Bell)

RIGHT
The German Army showed considerable interest in a modified Cobra II as a possible replacement for its anti-tank MBB Bo.105Ps (MBB)

BELOW RIGHT
The Model 249 in its 'PAH-2' configuration, with both Hellfire and TOW anti-tank missiles, 2.75 inch FFAR pods, and wing-tip mounted launch tubes for Stinger air-to-air missiles. Had the development been pursued, a full TADS/PNVS turret would have been fitted in place of the 20 mm gun (Bell)

if the Cobra II/Apache combination was such a good one. LHX is still unresolved even now, and the improved Cobra package remains on the shelf. It is interesting to note the comment made in Bell's brochure at the time, which underlined the fact that the proposed improvements '. . . aim at assuring effectiveness of the total (helicopter) force. While the AH-64/AH-1S 'hi-lo' mix presents a neat budgetary distinction, it is not reasonable to provide combat aviators in a common threat environment with a 'hi-lo' probability of survival.'

A further proposal was designed to meet the Army's Advanced Scout Helicopter (ASH) requirement, which called for an aircraft based on an existing airframe to replace the increasingly less capable and survivable OH-58 Kiowa. Again, the basis of the proposal was the multi-bladed Model 249. A whole range of new sensors and systems were to be provided, including the full Target Acquisition and Designation Sight/Pilot's Night Vision Sensor (TADS/PNVS) originally flown on the AH-64. An attractive feature of the programme was the airframe commonality that could be achieved—even more so if a derivative of the aircraft could be sold to other NATO nations. Apart from the rotor, the most fundamental departure from the basic Cobra layout was to be the deletion of the standard wing in favour of a 'mini-wing', designed to hold air-to-air and defence suppression (anti-radar) guided weapons. The ASH

Cobra would have been the first true 'fighter' helicopter, capable of taking-on other combat helicopters as well as ground-based missile systems.

Bell has always been interested in the European market for the Cobra, and the German Army's need to replace the anti-tank MBB Bo.105P (PAH-1 or *Panzerabwehr Hubschrauber* 1), offered the company an opportunity to encourage a little NATO commonality—never an easy thing to achieve at the best of times. The Germans needed well over 200 PAH-2s, and Bell realized that if they could be persuaded to favour the Model 249, it would add considerable weight to their proposals to the US Army. The German Army of course saw this equation the other way round, but the principle was the same.

The PAH-2 submission was the only 249 variant to result in any specific hardware, and even then it was only in representative form. The aircraft would incorporate a combination of many of the improvements suggested for the ASH programme, but it would retain the standard wing with full provision for TOW, Hellfire or any alternative European anti-tank weapon as primary armament. As in the ASH proposal, the inclusion of TADS/PNVS in the nose resulted in the deletion of the turret gun.

The 249 prototype was provided with a dummy nose section that could be interchanged with the gun turret, and it set off for European demonstration tour that included an appearance at the 1980 Farnborough

International display. The German Army evaluated the aircraft, along with a wide variety of other types including the AH-64, but eventually decided to design and build their own PAH-2 in partnership with the French, who by then were looking for a similar aircraft under the designation HAC (*Hélicoptère Anti-Char*). Despite an early agreement in principle between the two countries, the PAH-2/HAC programme took years to reach a technical consensus, and the first production aircraft will not see operational service until the late 1990s.

Unfortunately for Bell, the US Army also rejected the multi-bladed Cobra. The whole ASH programme was eventually dropped in favour of the less ambitious Army Helicopter Improvement Program (AHIP), which resulted in the company securing a contract to modify and update nearly 600 early OH-58 Kiowas to a new OH-58D standard. The 'Delta' aircraft features a night-capable, mast-mounted sight and a four-bladed composite rotor system.

Advanced Rotorcraft Technology Integration (ARTI)

During 1982 the US Army asked all appropriate manufacturers of helicopters and attack avionics to consider the requirements of the LHX programme.

ABOVE
The 'redundant' Model 249 was converted into a research vehicle for the US Army's Advanced Rotorcraft Technology Integration (ARTI) programme. As can be seen from this picture, the aircraft can be safely flown 'hands off' even close to the ground (Bell)

RIGHT
The Model 249 is still being improved and updated, and the next stage of the ARTI programme will concentrate on cockpit displays and sighting systems (Bell)

LHX was to perform scout/attack (Scat) and utility roles, be capable of single-pilot attack missions beyond the forward line of battle, and weigh no more than 8500 lb (later amended to 9500 lb). More than 5000 of the new helicopters would be needed, to replace most of the Army's AH-1s, OH-6s, OH-58s and UH-1s.

Even with the present generation of helicopters, a two-man crew is considered essential to fly and fight the aircraft successfully. A single-pilot LHX is certain to need a lot more electronic systems and a high degree of cockpit automation, particularly in the fields of navigation, target acquisition, flight controls and defensive countermeasures. To enable the manufacturers to spread the risks of the overall project more evenly, the Army Aviation Systems Command initiated a separately funded Advanced Rotorcraft Technology Integration (ARTI) programme, which could address some of the newer technologies involved.

Following the award of contracts under the ARTI programme in December 1983, Bell teamed up with Sperry Flight Systems (responsible for cockpit displays and sub-system management), Honeywell (flight controls) and Texas Instruments (sensors and avionics integration), to produce a hands off, fly-by-wire control system, using the temporarily redundant Model 249 as the basis of the flight research effort.

A digital processor is used to input control commands, and the aircraft is capable of flying a wide range of manoeuvres fully automatically. This frees the pilot to concentrate on navigation, target acquisition and weapons management. On 26 February 1985, project pilot Tom Warren put the aircraft through an impressive range of 'hands off' flight profiles, including a 'pop-up' attack simulation to 50 feet, followed by a 90 degree turn, before manoeuvring to re-establish his original heading and height. Afterwards Warren was enthusiastic about the system's capabilities, commenting that the automatic control functions did a superb job of flying the aircraft, and that it 'handled and performed just like the system designers said it would', a capability that would 'go a long way in reducing pilot workload, particularly in the NOE environment'.

Much work still remains to be done on the aircraft. Bell is currently 'fine tuning' the system, and attention will soon turn to advanced cockpit displays, which will include colour and monochrome multi-function VDUs, and some form of helmet-mounted sight similar to the Integrated Helmet and Display Sighting Sub-system (IHADSS) now being used operationally on the AH-64 Apache. Further on-board systems will eventually link the digital control computer to navigational inputs from an automatic heading-reference system, doppler and a digital map, as well as handling target acquisition and automatic tracking through a FLIR sensor and targeting processor.

Development Workhorses

It will not have escaped the reader's attention that 70-16019, the airframe currently serving as the proof-of-concept demonstrator for the next generation of helicopters, began life as a standard US Army AH-1G before being modified to carry TOW missiles as an 'interim' AH-1Q. It then took part in the ICAM programme as the prototype AH-1S, and was further modified to prove the four-bladed rotor system as the one and only Model 249.

Much the same is true of 161022, which has been a

ABOVE
During the qualification trials of the Hellfire missile system in 1980, a pair of development Cobras were used as launch aircraft, alongside the AH-64 target designators. These trials eventually resulted in the conversion of one airframe to a fully Hellfire-capable JAH-1G standard (Bell)

RIGHT
The Airborne Laser Locator/Designator (ALLD) was a bulky piece of equipment that had to be pod-mounted under the Cobra's wing (via Aldo Zanfi).

US Marine Corps AH-1T, AH-1T+ and SuperCobra (AH-1W prototype) during its long life. Following its completion of the 'W' qualification, it will emerge from Bell's plant as the 4BW, which could result in the twin-engined variant taking on a new lease of life with a four-bladed rotor system.

The other ICAM airframe (the YAH-1R, 70-15936) has also continued to contribute to the overall development of the Cobra. Ever since the unsuccessful SMASH programme, efforts to perfect various 'bolt-on' sensors and designators have continued, and one of the earliest of these was a pod-mounted system called Airborne Laser Locator/Designator (ALLD).

The ALLD pod was carried on the starboard outer pylon (as was the SMASH moving target indicator), and contained an Aeronautic precision stabilized sight, an International Laser Systems designator/rangefinder, a Rockwell laser spot tracker, a FLIR-sensor from Texas Instruments and a Lear-Seigler

TV camera. The whole system was intended to give the Cobra a full night/adverse weather capability, which would include the facility to designate targets for remote laser-guided weapons. A number of pods were built by the Aeronautics Division of Philco-Ford, and most of the testing was completed in 1974. It was decided subsequently that a similar system could be built into the Cobra, rather than pod-mounted on the wing. Accordingly a movable 'eyeball' containing the sensors was grafted onto the nose of the aircraft, under the new acronym ATAFCS (Airborne Target Acquisition Fire Control System). One of the aircraft converted to carry the new system was the AH-1R.

During March 1976 US Army trials were conducted with the 155 mm M712 Copperhead cannon-launched, terminally guided projectile. This weapon can be fired from conventional artillery pieces, but is 'steerable' to within about a kilometre of its nominal aiming point by homing onto laser energy provided by a remote target designator. During early trials the Cobra was used as the designator aircraft. Some of this research would have been relevant to the ASH proposal, but by then the Army's attention was directed increasingly towards the forthcoming AAH/Hellfire combination.

As the AH-64 Apache (AAH) programme gathered pace, the Hellfire missile system reached operational maturity. In order to test its effectiveness under realistic conditions before embarking on full-scale production, an exhaustive series of trials was conducted between April and July 1980. The trials were run by the US Army's Combat Development Experimentation Command (CDEC), under the overall auspices of the Operational Test and Evaluation Agency. The ATAFCS Cobras were used throughout these trials as 'surrogate' AAHs, designating targets for two development AH-64s and two non-ATAFCS Cobras that were being used as launch aircraft.

The live-fire phase commenced on 1 July, and during the following two weeks a total of 33 missiles were fired in conditions designed to test all available launch modes. Very high rates of success were demonstrated from both types of aircraft, with firings by day and by night, through smoke and dust, with the launch aircraft manoeuvring, in adverse weather conditions and with direct sunlight in the seeker's field of view.

Although this work was essentially to support the Apache programme, the potential of a Hellfire/Cobra combination was not lost on Bell. One aircraft was subsequently configured as a fully Hellfire-capable machine, and designated JAH-1G during evaluation. The Army has shown no interest in converting to Hellfire, preferring to stick with the less costly TOW/Cobra formula, which seems to fit more neatly into the philosophy of a 'hi-lo' mix of assets. The USMC, on the other hand, has elected to make both missile systems available to its Cobras.

The movable 'eyeball' sensor-pack of the Airborne Target Acquisition Fire Control System (ATAFCS) was carried experimentally by a number of Cobras (US Army via Mike Verier)

ABOVE LEFT
As the AH-64 Apache programme began to mature,
exhaustive tests of the aircraft's Hellfire missile system were
carried out by the US Army's CDEC (McDonnell Douglas
Helicopters)

ABOVE
The ATAFCS Cobras were used during the Hellfire trials,
designating targets for the AH-64s (US Army via Mike
Verier)

LEFT
Trials of the Hellfire missile system on the AH-1J were
highly successful, and the USMC has now adopted the
weapon as an option for all its AH-1Ws (Bell)

Chapter 6
You don't have to be a Marine to resent being shot at!

The US Marine Corps initially displayed no more than an academic interest in the concept of an armed helicopter. Their mission was entirely different to that of the Army, and besides, the Army could not call on its own dedicated close air support in the form of powerful fixed-wing elements. The Marine function has always been to provide a sea-borne assault force, and it was assumed that if, for some reason, the Corps could not be supported by its own aircraft, it would certainly be within the range of protective naval gunfire. Either way, the purpose of the helicopter was to transport the ground troops and all their supplies to where they were needed, and to get them there as quickly as possible. Helicopters were looked upon solely as airborne trucks, leaving other elements to provide defensive fire.

There were also other reasons for the reluctance to overspecialize. The Marines have to be prepared for deployment to anywhere in the world, jungle or desert, arctic or equator, at any time. The multiplicity of equipment needed for this role has inevitably stretched the budget almost to breaking point from time to time, leaving little room for the 'unnecessary luxury' of combat helicopters.

For sound tactical reasons the arming of existing types was also seen as a non-starter. In the era of the piston-engined UH-34 (formerly HUS-1) payloads were very limited, and every machine-gun bolted onto the aircraft meant one less Marine inside. Also, the only sensible place to mount a gun on the 'Huss' was in the single door, and this would certainly slow down the egress of troops at a time when the helicopter is at its most vulnerable—on the ground at a disputed landing zone. Finally, and probably the most powerful argument against the armed helicopter, was the widespread feeling that specialized types of this kind would reduce the available budget for fixed-wing aircraft, and perhaps put pressure on the Corps' already limited transport assets.

In March 1962, two decisions were made that ultimately brought about a change in doctrine, and led to the acceptance by the Marines of the attack helicopter elements we know today. On 1 March, the Secretary of the Navy approved the adoption of Bell's UH-1B for light reconnaissance and utility duties. The Marine aircraft was designated UH-1E, and it differed from its Army counterpart in having a rotor brake, naval avionics and communications equipment, and a basic structure consisting of aluminium, rather than the magnesium alloys used on the land-based Hueys, which are susceptible to salt-water corrosion. To avoid any need for structural redesigning, the weapons mounts incorporated by the Army were left in the airframe, although they were not required by the Marines.

Only a few days after the approval of the Huey order, the US Joint Chiefs of Staff decided that a squadron of Marine Corps HUS-1 (UH-34) helicopters should be deployed to Vietnam, instead of an Army unit that was equipped with the less capable CH-21 Shawnee. Consequently, on 22 March, 1st MAW was ordered to prepare and deploy the squadron, under an operation code-named 'Shufly'.

The unit selected was HMM-362, commanded by Lt Col Archie J Clapp; it commenced operations from Soc Trang on 15 April 1962, and by 22 April the first aircraft had received combat damage.

It quickly became apparent that the transport helicopters would need to be accompanied by far more suppressive fire if they were to remain airworthy in any great numbers. Resources were already limited in Vietnam, and by July, Gen David M Shoup, Commandant of the Marine Corps, was asking the Chief of Naval Operations to furnish him with six T-28 aircraft for helicopter support duties (the use of

The first USMC Cobras—handed over in February 1969—were single-engined AH-1Gs, complete with their full Army communications fit (Bell)

Initial crew training for the Marines had to be done at the Hunter Army Airfield in Georgia, because all the logistic support for the AH-1G was based there. The early Marine aircraft were taken from an Army production batch, so they all retained Army serials (Bell)

jets was not politically acceptable at that time). The Joint Chief's procrastinated over the issue, because the rules of engagement then in force clearly stated that the enemy must fire first.

It was not until February 1963 that the JCS finally gave temporary permission for helicopter crews to shoot first, but even then they were only to open fire against 'clearly defined VC elements considered to be a threat to the helicopter and its passengers'. Less than a week later the Pentagon changed its mind, and everyone returned to a 'defence only' posture. This did not prevent the men of HMM-362 proudly announcing on 13 March that three of their UH-34s had, for the first time, successfully provided close air support during an assault landing.

Finally, after yet another request from Gen Shoup for armed T-28s, the 'Shufly' squadron was told that it would receive the support of six Army UH-1B gunships. The Hueys arrived in April 1963, and the Marine Corps was learning in the hardest way

possible that it did, after all, need armed helicopters.

While this was going on in Vietnam, early UH-1Es had been coming off the Bell production line. The first operational aircraft were handed over to VMO-1 at Fort Worth on 21 February 1964. Then, in May, as if to remind the Marines once more about the restrictive rules of engagement, the Joint Chiefs of Staff issued a statement underlining the fact that armed helicopters were not to be used as a substitute for close air support.

In August 1964 North Vietnamese fast patrol boats changed the entire nature of the war by attacking two American destroyers in the Gulf of Tonkin. These attacks opened the flood gates of US political frustration with the area, and within a few days men and materials were pouring into South Vietnam and preparing for a long fight. The then Commandant of the Marine Corps, Gen Greene, ordered high priority work to begin on an armament kit for the UH-34, and this was followed in October by a similar directive covering the UH-1E. By December 1964 the first TK-1 (Temporary Kit 1) sets were issued to the 'Shufly' squadron, and in January VMO-6 at Camp Pendleton had the TK-2 kits for its UH-1Es. Thanks to the unplanned (but undoubtedly fortuitous) existence of the airframe hardpoints, each Huey kit could be installed in less than a day without having to make any holes in the aircraft.

The armed UH-1E proved to be useful and effective, although in some ways its very success compounded the Marines' problems. The new aircraft were assigned to VMOs (squadrons whose duties were concerned with observation, forward air control and general liaison), but their constant involvement in escort missions placed tremendous pressures on these other resources. The planned arrival of the OV-10 Bronco in 1968 would go some way towards alleviating the problem, but there were already those within the USMC who could see that a fundamental shift in policy was needed. An incident that occurred during the late summer of 1967 illustrates just why the UH-1E was such a highly valued escort.

On 19 August that year, Capt Stephen W Pless of VMO-6, was flying his Huey gunship as chase aircraft for an emergency Medevac in southern Quang Ngai Provence. He heard over the radio net that four US Army soldiers were stranded on a beach to the north of Duc Pho, and were about to be overwhelmed by a large enemy force. He flew to the scene immediately, and found about 60 Vietcong out in the open, some of them beating and bayoneting the downed Americans. Without further thought he attacked the enemy troops, killing and wounding many of them, and driving the survivors into the tree line with machine-gun fire and rockets delivered from such low altitude that the aircraft was pelted with fragments from its own exploding ordnance.

Still under heavy small-arms fire, Capt Pless landed between the communists and the wounded soldiers, and his two crewmen, Gunnery Sgt Leroy N Poulson and L/Cpl John G Phelps, disembarked to help the men aboard. The co-pilot, Capt Rupert E Fairfield Jnr, killed three nearby VC with a burst from an M-60, then ran to help the crewmen while Pless brought the aircraft to the hover and again directed fire at the enemy in the trees. Eventually the wounded were all taken aboard the helicopter, and Pless headed out to sea. With eight men and full combat ordnance on board, the UH-1 was heavily overloaded, and so sluggish that it settled into the water four times. Pless managed to skip it back into the air on each occasion, while the crew jettisoned all unnecessary weight until enough altitude could be gained to enable the Huey to limp back to the 1st Hospital Company's landing pad at Chu Lai.

Apart from the rescue itself, the crew were credited with 20 confirmed and 38 probable enemy dead. Fairfield, Poulson and Phelps each received the Navy Cross, and Capt Pless was awarded the Medal of Honor, for an action that the citation rightly described as 'above and beyond the call of duty'.

Eventually the pace and scope of operations in SE Asia, coupled with the obvious success of the Army's Cobras, convinced the Marines that dedicated combat helicopters were now vital to the war effort.

They particularly wanted a twin-engined aircraft, equipped with a rotor brake and naval avionics. It would also need a bigger turret-gun in order to increase the stand-off range, because sea-borne assaults would not have the natural ground-cover advantage enjoyed by the Army.

It is beyond the scope of this narrative to record the political in-fighting that surrounded this acquisition. Bell was more than happy to provide a twin-engined aircraft, but it would have been expensive for a small production run, and the only really suitable powerplant was built in Canada. This unhappy combination delayed the project so much that the USMC eventually had to accept 38 Army-standard AH-1Gs in order to get something into service as quickly as possible. The aircraft were funded from the FY 1969 budget, but the Marines continued to press for the increased safety of two engines.

In February 1969 the first Marine Corps Cobras were handed over by Bell, and after the brief ceremony they were flown straight to Hunter Army Airfield, Georgia, where they were to be used for aircrew training. Three months later, out of a mixed Army and Marine class of 39 students, the four USMC pilots on the course graduated in the first four places.

The Command Chronology for VMO-2 records laconically that: 'The first Marine Corps AH-1G in Vietnam went operational 18 April 1969.' Four aircraft had been flown out aboard US Air Force transports a week or so earlier, and after reassembly and testing, they began operations from the Marble Mountain Air Facility in Da Nang. The first actual mission was a Medevac escort flown by Maj Donald E P Miller (later to become the Commanding General of 3rd MAW), with 1st Lt Tommy L James in the front seat.

During the ensuing months VMO-2 received a total of 12 AH-1Gs, and the aircraft continued to give a good account of itself, although it was hampered by the Army communications fit and some difficulty in obtaining spares. Despite the fact that it clearly needed a 20 mm gun, the Marines took to the aircraft just as their Army counterparts had. The lack of a rotor brake was acceptable for land-based missions, but it made shipboard operations much more difficult.

While VMO-2 was deploying its first few Cobras, Bell was flying the prototype Model 212, which had been developed for (and jointly funded by) the Canadian Government. This was a twin-engined version of the Huey, powered by an arrangement of two Canadian-built Pratt & Whitney PT6T engines driving a common output shaft. A subsequent large order for the aircraft for the Canadian Armed Forces was more than matched by a US Government purchase of 212s (UH-1Ns) to equip US Navy, Air Force and Marine units. This early 'offset' deal had removed the political objection to using foreign-made engines in helicopters for the US armed services, and established a link with the Canadians that would

eventually succeed in providing the Marine Corps with its coveted twin-engined Cobra.

Following the Tet Offensive in Vietnam, the Marine Corps resorted to a persuasive argument known as the 'attrition buy'. Broadly speaking, this strategy suggested that if helicopters had to be ordered anyway (to make up for combat losses), they might as well be the more survivable twin-engined variant. This pressure initially referred to the replacement of downed Hueys, but the logic of the argument applied equally well to the Cobra— especially as the twin-pack powerplant had now been proved with the Huey rotor system, and was finally clear of the political log-jam that had prevented an earlier Cobra conversion.

The pace of development during the SE Asia conflict made the unveiling of new types at Fort Worth something of a routine for Bell, but the October 1969 ceremony to hand over the first twin-engined AH-1J SeaCobra to the US Marine Corps was more significant than usual. Although nobody could see it at the time, this was to be the point at which the Cobra family diverged along two very different paths. The US Department of Defense had finally been persuaded by the case put forward by the Marines, and had agreed to fund the development of the 'twin-pac' aircraft. The machine itself was a great leap forward in capability over the original Cobra, and it provided Bell with the opportunity to produce even more powerful and effective variants.

Seventeen years later this process of evolution was to culminate in another ceremony on the same flight line: the first delivery of the awesome AH-1W 'SuperCobra'.

Apart from the new engine installation, the

AH-1J was structurally unchanged from the 'Army' AH-1G. The Marine aircraft was powered by two Pratt & Whitney (United Aircraft of Canada Ltd) T400-CP-400 turboshaft engines which were mounted side by side and permanently coupled, driving a single output shaft through a combining gearbox. In addition to gaining 400 shp over the AH-1G's Lycoming T53, the new arrangement conferred true twin-engined reliability—a great asset in combat or during long over-water missions. As the rotor and drive system were almost unchanged, the 'J' model was transmission limited, which meant that the two engines could produce more power than the drive train was designed to handle. This provided a useful margin for single-engined hovering, and allowed more operational flexibility in 'hot and high' conditions. The AH-1J was marginally heavier empty than the 'G' model, but it retained the overall 10,000 lb gross weight limit.

Designed from the outset for shipboard operations,

RIGHT
The AH-1J was the first Cobra variant to field the M-197 20 mm turret gun (Mike Verier)

the AH-1J had the long-awaited rotor brake, and was fully equipped with naval avionics and radios. Critical components in a number of areas were also changed as a protection against saline corrosion—a very real problem on board ship.

The AH-1J also represented a milestone in Cobra development as the first variant to field the M-197 20 mm turret gun. Apart from the new gun, the initial weapons capability of the aircraft was the same as that of earlier versions, although it was subsequently cleared to carry a much wider variety of ordnance than the Army machines—a reflection of the more diverse nature of Marine operations. Some of the later AH-1Js were fitted with revised weapons pylons and a ballistic canopy ejection system. Although these two modifications added another 100 lb or so to the empty weight of the aircraft, they were considered generally worthwhile and eventually retro-fitted to the entire fleet. A number of minor equipment and systems changes have been made over the years, but basically the Marine aircraft is the same today as it was in the early 1970s. Most of them have already been replaced in active service by the re-engined AH-1W (see Chapter 10), but even as a Reserve aircraft, the Sidewinder and Hellfire capable AH-1J will provide a formidable back-up should the need ever arise.

Operational at last

Unlike the 'G' models which had required no pre-service testing by the Marines, the AH-1J was considered to be a new aircraft, and the first four were consigned in July 1970 to the Naval Air Test Center at Patuxent River, Maryland, for an exhaustive evaluation. The next seven airframes—still lacking some components that were yet to be fitted by Bell—began to arrive in September at MCAS New River, North Carolina, for air and ground crew training.

In January 1971, as preparations were being made to deploy the first AH-1Js to Vietnam, 1st Lt J W Gallo of HML-367 was celebrating the fact that he had become the first Marine aviator to complete 1000 hours on the AH-1G. HML-367 was shortly to begin participation in 'Lam Son 719'.

'Lam Son' was intended as a blocking operation to counter a suspected North Vietnamese assault through neighbouring Laos. Its objective was to cut the infamous Ho Chi Min Trail by seizing Tchepone, and denying the enemy his supplies. It was also designed as a major test of the 'Vietnamization' of the war, in that only South Vietnamese ground troops

Marine Corps Cobras are cleared to carry a larger range of weapons than their Army counterparts. This display includes a variety of bombs, and the huge CBU-55 fuel/air explosive which is used for the instant clearance of landing grounds. In addition to the items shown here, the aircraft now carries TOW and Hellfire missiles, as well as Sidewinders and Sidearms (USMC)

would be used—the American participation was to be limited to providing transport and fire support from the air. D day was set for 6 February 1971.

The operation unleashed one of the biggest combined US Army and Marine helicopter forces used during the entire war—over 650 machines were committed to the action. HML-367's Cobras were immediately in the thick of it, flying escorts to CH-53 lifts into Khe Sahn. Just over a week later, while increasingly bitter fighting raged over the Trail, US Air Force C-133 transports landed at Da Nang carrying the first four AH-1Js. Two days earlier Col 'Tiny' Nieson had arrived at the Marble Mountain air base with a team of eight pilots and 23 enlisted men. They were all freshly qualified on the new SeaCobra, and tasked with preparing it for combat evaluation as quickly as possible.

The 'Lam Son' operation lasted just over six weeks, and by the time it was over the AH-1Js had certainly proved their worth. The brief evaluation period ended on 28 April, having accumulated some 614 hours in the air. During this time the four aircraft fired 14,950 rounds of 7.62 mm Minigun ammunition, and 72,945 rounds from the longer-range 20 mm gun— showing a marked combat preference for the M-197. They also launched 2842 2.75 inch rockets, and a variety of other ordnance.

Despite its fierce introduction to combat, the AH-1J was not destined to remain land-based in Vietnam for long. US forces had already begun to disengage from SE Asia, and even before 'Lam Son' the USMC helicopter contingent had been reduced to seven squadrons. These were further depleted when four CH-46 units withdrew during March and April 1971, leaving the three remaining squadrons to continue operations until they too were withdrawn in June.

In June 1972 the AH-1J returned to combat operations in an action code-named MARHUK (see Chapter 8), and eight aircraft made a brief appearance at the end of April 1975, when they acted as escorts to the transport elements of Operation 'Frequent Wind'—the frantic effort to evacuate US staff and their dependants from Saigon before it was finally overrun by NVA troops. Both of these actions were conducted by HMA-369 from the decks of US Navy assault ships.

Apart from a new paint scheme and a few minor equipment changes, the USMC's AH-1Js have remained virtually the same as they were in the early 1970s (Mike Verier)

Chapter 7
The King is Dead – Long Live the King

The Model 309 KingCobra has remained a relatively unknown project, primarily because only two prototypes were built. The fact that the aircraft failed to reach production belies the importance of the programme in terms of the effect it was to have on Cobra development as a whole.

The decision to proceed with the construction of the prototypes was partially prompted by the difficulties encountered by the Lockheed AH-56 Cheyenne. Bell was not alone in the industry in suspecting that cost escalations and complexity would eventually kill the Cheyenne, and Sikorsky was known to be working on the S-67 Blackhawk project as a private venture replacement for the AAFSS programme.

Bell had initiated several studies of the requirements of a second generation attack helicopter, and during the period from 1969 to 1971 a multitude of design ideas emerged from the projects office. Some of these were destined to go no further than the drawing or model stage, but others were developed into hardware and test-flown. The company's design engineers were certain that they could offer the Army

RIGHT
The Lockheed AH-56 Cheyenne proved to be a costly mistake. The original specification was far too advanced, and the whole AAFSS programme was eventually cancelled (Lockheed via Aldo Zanfi)

ABOVE RIGHT
This dive-brake 'umbrella' was one of the many ideas listed in Bell's own archives as being connected with the KingCobra programme. Seen here mounted on a standard Army Cobra, the device is clearly designed to fold into the sleeve provided, leaving the central core as a streamlined plug. How successful the arrangement was is unknown, but it was never applied to any production aircraft (Bell)

a useful increase in capability, while keeping the costs well below those of the full AAFSS specification. It also seemed logical to add all the improvements to the twin-engined 'Marine' aircraft, which would open up an even bigger market.

As is usual with projects of this kind, the financing of the demonstrators was shared between Bell (as 'prime contractor') and a number of component and systems suppliers. Every company involved was chasing the same potential market for the fully integrated weapons system, and it was in their mutual interest to make the aircraft as combat-efficient as possible. The airframe itself, while of primary importance, was really only a vehicle to carry all the sub-systems and ordnance.

After agreeing finally all the teaming arrangements, Bell committed itself to the construction of two prototypes, one to represent the twin-engined 'Marine' variant, and the other a single-engined 'Army' version. The decision to launch the project

was announced in January 1971, just as the first AH-1Js were being prepared for their deployment to Vietnam. The first KingCobra—the twin-engined machine—made its maiden flight on 10 September, less than nine months after the start of the programme.

The aircraft was formally unveiled to the world's press and a number of high-ranking military delegations on 28 September 1971. The presentation contained more than a little 'showbiz', as Gene Colvin, Bell's project pilot for the Model 309, held the aircraft in the hover one and a half miles or so from the gathering, shielded by trees and apparently unseen. At the appropriate moment he performed a 100 foot 'pop-up' manoeuvre, and then carried out a simulated high-speed gun-run, directly towards the suitably impressed audience.

Following this piece of pure theatre, a slightly more restrained presentation of the aircraft's military capabilities was completed, and this was backed up by a hangar display which involved exhibits from all the main sub-contractors and included a full-scale mock-up of an AAFSS-configured aircraft. During this exhibition the USMC guests were presented with an 18-page brochure describing a whole range of optional improvements that could enhance the combat performance of their AH-1Js.

During the launch celebrations, a brief ceremony was also held to present Bell's first proof-of-concept armed helicopter, the Model 207 Sioux Scout, to Gen William J Maddox, the then Director of Army Aviation. He received the aircraft on behalf of the Army Aviation Museum at Fort Rucker, where it can still be seen today.

The first KingCobra clearly displayed its SeaCobra origins, but it was a very different animal to the operational AH-1J. Structurally it had a toughened airframe to cope with much higher gross weights, and the tail boom had been lengthened and fitted with a new ventral fin, both to improve directional stability and to make provision for the increased diameter of the rotor (48 feet). The main rotor itself featured a new high-lift aerofoil section developed by the German aerodynamicist, Prof Franz X Wortman. Compared to the standard blade, it had a wider chord and an asymmetric section. The rotor also had what at the time were very odd-looking forward-swept tips, designed to delay the onset of compressibility and reduce the distinctive thudding beat that always heralded the arrival of any member of the Huey family.

The prototype aircraft was powered by the same T400-CP-400 'twin pac' shaft turbines as the standard 'J' model, but a strengthened drive-train avoided the need to de-rate their combined output

The twin-engined Model 309 KingCobra flew for the first time on 10 September 1971, just nine months after construction began (Bell)

LEFT
The TOW-armed KingCobra prototype performed a dramatic 'pop-up' manoeuvre, before completing a simulated gun-run towards the guests at its formal unveiling (Bell)

RIGHT
The original Model 207 Sioux Scout now resides in the Army Aviation Museum at Fort Rucker. Six small air-to-surface rockets can just be seen beneath each stub wing (Mike Verier)

BELOW
The KingCobra, seen here on the right alongside a standard AH-1G, was equipped with a new rotor of much wider chord and incorporating swept-forward tips (Bell)

LEFT
The KingCobra's 'visionics' turret was basically the bottom half of the AH-56 Cheyenne system (Bell)

BELOW
AH-1J 3-4407 of the Iranian Imperial Army seen in about 1976 (Bell via Robert F Dorr)

BELOW RIGHT
The single-engined 'Army' version of the KingCobra was flown for the first time in January 1972. The aircraft was powered by a Lycoming T55-L-7C, flat-rated to provide 2000 shp (Bell)

power. The AH-IJ was transmission-limited to 1250 shp for take-off, but the KingCobra used the transmission system originally developed for the HueyTug (a specialized 'flying crane' variant of the UH-1C), which allowed the aircraft to absorb the powerplant's full 1800 shp. Later versions were planned with engines of 1970 shp, and consideration was being given to the eventual possibility of reaching 2400 shp after some development of the transmission.

The KingCobra had grown a large, bulged housing under the belly, and a prominent nasal extension carrying the 'visonics' turret. Both of these illustrated the Bell philsophy of utilizing existing hardware whenever possible. The bulge housed a new high capacity 20 mm ammunition drum, which was originally a shortened, but otherwise quite standard, unit from an F-111 fighter-bomber. The sighting turret was actually the bottom half of the AH-56 system. Unlike Lockheed, Bell had decided not to use the complete turntable-mounted sight and seat which could track targets through a full 360 degrees. This was done primarily to save weight and complexity, although it had been reported that gunners using the Cheyenne system were often suffering from third degree vertigo by the time they had tracked through 180 degrees, due to the disparity between the visual and physical inputs they were receiving!

The potential weapons capability of the KingCobra was also greatly enhanced. Encounters in Vietnam with an enemy that regularly deployed heavy calibre anti-aircraft artillery and heat-seeking missiles, had already confirmed that NOE tactics and a greater stand-off range would be essential if the attack helicopter was to stand any chance of survival in the anti-armour role. The first demonstration aircraft retained the FFARs and the proven M-197 20 mm turret gun, but it also carried mock-ups of the now standard TOW missile launchers. The wing-tip mounting of air-to-air self-defence missiles such as Sidewinder or a modified Stinger was seen as a possibility, and future developments could have included provision for the Hellfire anti-armour weapon, medium range attack missiles (MRAMs), or a version of the high-speed anti-radiation missile (HARM).

The US Marine Corps was very enthusiastic about the increased capability offered by the 'Improved SeaCobra' package, but in the light of the omnipresent budgetary restrictions it was clear that only parts of the system could be afforded. No such financial restraints applied to the Shah of Iran however, and when a contract was signed just over a year later, the aircraft he wanted was a twin-engined AH-IJ incorporating a whole range of features validated by the KingCobra. That order represented the largest ever US export sale of helicopters.

The single-engined 'Army' version of the KingCobra flew some four months after its twin-engined sister ship. Structurally it was identical to the first airframe. Both aircraft had been built to

production (not fabrication) type drawings, and it was possible to utilize standard AH-1 jigs and tooling during their assembly—which at least indicated that a retro-fit programme was entirely feasible if required.

The powerplant for the second aircraft was a Lycoming T55-L-7C. Capable of delivering 2850 shp in its unmodified form, the engine for the KingCobra was flat-rated to provide 2000 shp at 4000 feet and 95°F. This allowed the aircraft to hover out of ground effect under those conditions, even at its normal take-off weight of about 14,000 lb. This clear improvement in performance brought previously marginal 'hot and high' operations well within its capabilities.

The single-engined machine was always intended to be fully instrumented and equipped to military standards. It is worth looking at some of the sub-systems in detail, because a number of the capabilities demonstrated by the aircraft are only just becoming widely available today. In the early 1970s the only people who had 'sensors' of sufficient reliability and accuracy to be of any real use to the military were the entirely fictional crew of the *other* USS *Enterprise*!

Aside from the powerplant suppliers, the major sub-contractors to the programme were as follows:

General Electric	Primary fire-control system and gunner's sighting station, laser rangefinder, HUD and computer (Burlington Vermont also handled the 20 mm gun system)
Litton Guidance & Control	Inertial navigator and fire control
Sperry Univac	Helmet Sighting System
Dalmo Victor	Pilot's Night Vision System (LLTV)
Honeywell	Radar altimeter
Itek	Radar Warning System
Texas Instruments	FLIR night vision system
Hughes Aircraft	TOW missile system

The heart of the KingCobra weapons system was the Stabilized Multi-sensor Sight (SMS), which combined with a fire control computer to display targeting information through both the gunner/co-pilot's TSU

This picture of the twin-engined KingCobra shows the aircraft configured for battle. The weapons include a 19-shot FFAR-pod, a quad TOW launcher, and the 20 mm rotary cannon. The pilot's LLTV system is derived from a camera housed in the pylon, immediately above and behind the cockpit (Bell)

and the pilot's HUD. Both crewmen had helmet-mounted sights to assist rapid target acquisition with the turret gun and SMS.

The SMS itself featured a stabilized mirror and optical bench. Mounted on the bench were day and night optics, a neodymium laser-rangefinder/designator, the FLIR system and the TOW missile tracker. The FLIR—which is still not fitted to operational Cobras—displayed at +2 or +6 magnification in the gunner's eyepiece and, if required, on the pilot's HUD. Operating in the far infra-red region, it could give a high-resolution picture in total darkness, or be used to penetrate light fog and smoke during daylight: in either mode it could easily reveal camouflaged vehicles that would be invisible to the naked eye.

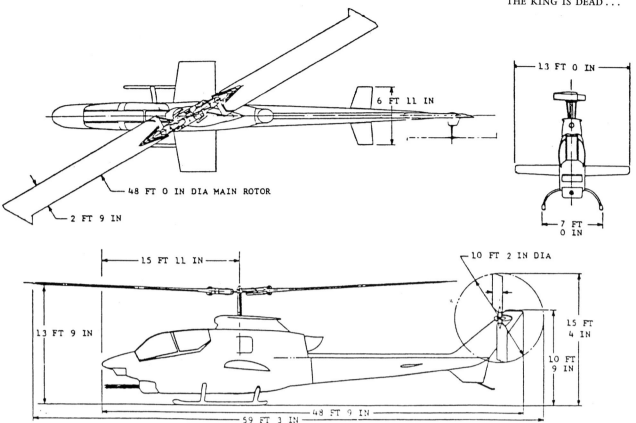

6 FT 11 IN

48 FT 0 IN DIA MAIN ROTOR

2 FT 9 IN

13 FT 0 IN

7 FT 0 IN

15 FT 11 IN

10 FT 2 IN DIA

13 FT 9 IN

15 FT 4 IN

10 FT 9 IN

48 FT 9 IN

59 FT 3 IN

LEFT
The 'big wing' KingCobra was only prepared in mock-up form, but the production version would have provided an extra 500 lb of fuel capacity, and additional weapons station space (at the tips) for air-to-air missiles such as Redeye or Stinger. The Wortmann rotor has by now been deleted (Bell)

ABOVE
Three-view drawing showing the dimensions of the proposed 'big wing' KingCobra in its single-engined form (Bell)

The pilot was provided with an independent low-light TV system to enable him to fly the aircraft in almost total darkness, even though the gunner was using the FLIR targeting sensor. The forward-facing camera was mounted in the 'sail' above and behind the rear cockpit, and its optical system was capable of automatically resolving detail in any conditions from starlight to bright sunlight. The resulting picture was displayed on the pilot's HUD.

Navigation was centred on the Litton inertial navigation system (INS), which could be updated from the Doppler to give the pilot his precise current location, and provide bearing and range information for any one of up to 16 preset locations. The INS also provided primary attitude references to the gunner, the fire control computer and the TOW electronics. Other nav-related systems included a VHF/FM homer, an ADF, and IFF transponders, a radar-

altimeter with low-altitude warning, and a standby gyromagnetic compass. The combination of equipment was carefully chosen to give the aircraft an unprecedented ability to find and attack its targets in the most adverse of conditions. The communications suite covered UHF/AM, VHF/AM, and VHF/FM, with provision for an HF SSB radio and the KY-28 secure voice system.

As originally conceived, the KingCobra was to feature a number of refinements that were either not pursued, or which fell by the wayside during development. This has led over the years to some disparity between published descriptions and the aircraft itself. Chief amongst these was the so-called 'big wing'. With a span of 13 feet and much greater chord than the original, the new wing was intended to be 'wet' and thereby increase the fuel capacity by some 500 lb, raising the overall total to 2300 lb. It also provided greater clearance for the inboard weapons pylons, which meant that a jamming pod—possibly the AN/ALQ 87—could be pylon-mounted on the 'corner' of the fuselage between the skids. (Bell drawings show the pod on either side, depending on their date.) Hardpoints were to be incorporated at the tips of the new wing to provide additional weapons stations. Concurrent with the introduction of the big wing, the tail rotor was to be returned to the port side of the fin. Photographs are published here for the first time showing what is believed to be a mock-up of the wing fitted to the twin-engined KingCobra, but in the event the development was not pursued.

Chapter 8
MARHUK

As 1971 drew to a close the American war effort in Vietnam was being scaled down. President Nixon was under considerable pressure from a strong anti-war movement, whose increasingly violent demonstrations, fuelled by obviously hostile media reporting of almost every aspect of the war, had forced him into conceding the total withdrawal of US forces at the earliest possible opportunity.

The 'Lam Son' incursion, whatever its actual results, had been portrayed to the world at large as a military débacle—despite the fact that it probably delayed the invasion of South Vietnam by at least twelve months. Nevertheless, even in the face of such intense criticism of the policy, an increasing dependence on the 'Vietnamization' of the war was seen as the only practical way out of the dilemma, and with this in mind the President confirmed in January 1972 that US troop withdrawals would continue.

Meanwhile, the peace talks in Paris continued to produce absolutely no concessions from the North Vietnamese, who seemed to have all the time in the world and no intention of giving even the slightest ground. They had failed to win a military victory in the accepted sense of the word, but they were slowly achieving a complete political victory. The American public wanted an end to the war at virtually any price, and the communists knew it.

When the big attack on South Vietnam did come on 30 March 1972, it was called the 'Easter Offensive' by a world that seemed unwilling to recognize it as a full-scale invasion. Consequently, a month later, Nixon was still pushing for an orderly withdrawal, while the Paris talks were completely stalled and the North Vietnamese Army was making steady progress.

As the ground troops left, the US Navy and Air Force were tasked with assisting the beleaguered South Vietnamese troops. Even B-52 strategic bombers were used in an uncharacteristic tactical role as part of their 'Arc Light' mission programme. Due

to their capability of laying down heavy, concentrated bomb patterns, they met with some success. On one occasion in mid-May the B-52s caught hundreds of NVA troops out in the open at An Loc, and caused massive enemy casualties whilst bombing at times less than 700 yards away from the friendly forces.

President Nixon, and his chief negotiator at the Paris talks, Henry Kissinger (later to become US Secretary of State), finally realized that the communists had no intention of negotiating seriously, and concluded that while US troop withdrawals should continue, the time had come to put direct military pressure on the North. Accordingly, on 8 May 1972, the mining of Hanoi and six other ports and harbours was ordered, in an attempt to disrupt the flow of *materiel* that the North needed to continue the war. An important part of this campaign of disruption was to involve the Cobra.

An operation initiated in June 1972 was known by the acronym MARHUK (derived from MARine HUnter/Killer). At the time the operation was highly secret because it involved the interdiction of supplies being landed from third-country (i.e., non-belligerent) merchant ships, and was therefore politically sensitive in the extreme. The records of these missions have only recently been de-classified, and details of the operation are recounted here for the first time outside USMC publications.

MARHUK came about because it was necessary to carry out surveillance and interdiction on the Hon La anchorage in North Vietnam. The US fixed-wing assets and aircraft carriers were all heavily committed to operations further south, offering as much air

The Marines had always seen the Cobra as part of a combined assault team, and its primary task was to provide protection to the transport elements. This doctrine was temporarily abandoned for the MARHUK missions (Frank B Mormillo)

support as possible to the battered South Vietnamese forces. The Cobra was an ideal alternative weapons platform, because it could operate from a non-aviation ship (i.e., not a carrier), and was sufficiently well armed to find and destroy the sort of small lighters being used for the ship-to-shore transfer of supplies.

Accordingly it fell to the men of the newly-formed HMA-369 to use the Cobra as a light attack aircraft for the first time. It should be remembered that this was against the doctrine of the Marine Corps, which saw the AH-1J as part of a combined assault team—certainly not in a role more suited to a fixed-wing aircraft. This meant that Maj Hansen and his men were going to have to write their own tactics manual as they went along; a challenge that they willingly accepted.

The Hon La anchorage is a relatively small area of water, sheltered by three offshore islands, with the coastline forming the third side of a pocket. At the time, all three sides of the pocket were defended by a considerable collection of anti-aircraft weapons, ranging from .51 calibre up to 57 mm. It was inside this area that operations had to be conducted. An associated beachline extended some 10 nm each side of the anchorage, and this too constituted a threat.

The vessels used as base ships for the MARHUK missions were all flag-configured 'Austin' class amphibious transport docks (LPDs). These assault ships had an aft flightdeck, below which was a well-dock intended for the deployment of landing craft. They were a comparatively new class (construction having begun in 1965), displacing some 16,000 tons fully loaded, and similar in many respects to the Royal Navy's 'Fearless' class assault ships. The fact that they were 'flag-configured' meant that they were, in effect, command ships, equipped with the necessary radar and electronic systems to enable a flag-officer to co-ordinate an action involving a number of other ships. The squadron complement was to be seven AH-1Js and 18 pilots, this being largely determined by the 'spotting' limitations imposed by the small size of the deck, and the obvious precaution that an armed aircraft needed to be parked in such a way that any inadvertent discharge of ordnance was aimed outboard.

HMA-369 had a busy few months immediately before departure. Located at MCAS Futenma on Okinawa, the squadron was having some difficulty in maintaining its full complement of pilots, especially after suffering a mass rotation of the personnel who had delivered the first AH-1Js some months earlier. However, a combination of pilot training (despite at one stage being reduced to only two aircraft) and the gradual arrival of already qualified people, ensured that the unit continued to work up to full strength. The arrival in mid-May of four new Cobras—flown to Futenma by C-5A—greatly assisted matters.

On 12 June the squadron got word of its possible deployment. Message traffic later that afternoon suggested that departure would be required in less than two days, so embarkation procedures were cranked up. On 14 June two Cobras, with their pilots and ground crews, returned from temporary detachment to other units, bringing HMA-369's strength up to eight aircraft. Maj Hansen formally assumed command the following day.

The squadron finally embarked on USS *Denver* (LPD-9) on 16 June, minus one aircraft that had suffered mechanical problems. The ship sailed immediately, and the crews lost no time in commencing their day and night carrier qualifications, and studying an assortment of briefings and intelligence material that had been prepared for them. They were virtually given a free hand as far as the development of tactics was concerned, and their mission was broadly defined to include 'visual surveillance, photographic reconnaissance, target ordnance delivery, and the control of fixed-wing aircraft strikes (now known as the 'FACA/TACA' mission)'.

The Command Chronology for the period records

During the MARHUK operations HMA-369 had a complement of only seven AH-1Js. This particular example 157781) was flown by Lt (now Col) David C Corbett, USMC. The aircraft was finished overall in a well weathered FS14097 Field green, with all the markings in white or black as shown. The tail band was yellow with red 'danger' arrow and black lettering, but the national insignia was toned down, leaving only the red central bar. Most of the safety markings (RESCUE access, etc) were not toned down. The tail rotor was Olive drab with yellow tips, and the tail skid was striped red and yellow (Mike Verier)

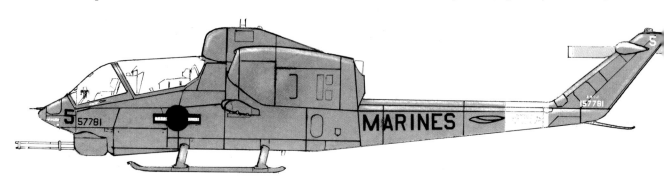

An AH-1J photographed during the MARHUK missions. The 'tone down' operation appears to have been concerned with hiding the national identity of the aircraft, rather than with effective camouflage. The US insignia is virtually painted out, while the yellow safety markings compete for attention with glossy white rocket pods (Col D Corbett via Bryan Wilburn)

in the usual clipped style, '20 June 1972. HMA-369 arrived on station in the Gulf of Tonkin for participation in Operation Linebacker, MARHUK mission.' Two days later the first mission, MARHUK 1, was flown, and the record coldly states that 'ordnance was expended on designated targets'.

The first task the squadron faced was the observation of activity in the anchorage, which at the time of MARHUK 1's arrival was centred around a Chinese Communist merchant ship. This 'snooping' provoked shore batteries to open fire on the reconnaissance aircraft—an action they quickly regretted, because it brought a swift and aggressive response from the Cobras.

Things really began to pop during a visit from the 'brass' on 1 July. During this period, radar detected a group of small lighters leaving the vicinity of the merchantman and heading rapidly south. A flight of two Cobras was vectored onto them, and the pair inflicted severe damage on the formation, leaving twelve boats either destroyed or heavily damaged. Shoreline defences opened up on the Cobras, who returned fire with considerable effect, destroying at least one .51 calibre emplacement and damaging another.

Operations continued on a daily basis, with 'Pistol Pete' (squadron callsign) flights engaged on photo-mapping the entire operational area, as well as attacking anything that came off a ship. On 8 July an apparently unguided ballistic rocket was fired at one flight from the shoreline. It missed its mark, but it heralded another increase in the growing weight of

ordnance being hurled at the Cobras (it was later concluded that this was an SA-7 'Strella', the first of many to be fired at, and miss, the MARHUKers).

On 12 July the first damage from hostile fire was recorded, albeit of a minor nature. Later that day 'Pistol Pete' aircraft flew the first night mission of the MARHUK series, making their observations with the aid of starshells fired from accompanying destroyers. These night flights were sometimes subjected to attack from 37 mm positions around the anchorage, and whilst such contact was normally avoided, the night of 18 July saw a Cobra return fire on one AAA position, causing several secondary explosions.

A second Chinese ship entered the anchorage on 25 July, and aircraft were immediately launched to photograph and observe the new arrival. Operations against its cargo however, had to be delayed, because USS *Denver* was due for replenishment in port, and she left the area the following day, bound for Subic Bay in the Philippines. After a brief stay at the nearby NAS Cubi Point, the Cobras were flown aboard USS *Cleveland* (LPD-7), which was dispatched immediately to Hon La, arriving there on 4 August in foul weather that would prevent flying for another two days.

Operations were then geared to continuous night-time surveillance, with daylight attacks on random targets-of-opportunity. These tactics culminated in what the squadron report describes as a 'mini war' on 17 August, involving attacks on the anchorage installations and other designated targets by both naval gunfire and fixed-wing strike aircraft. All target spotting and forward air control tasks were carried out by the Cobras, who were able to direct fire accurately onto both predetermined and opportunity targets.

After an enforced break in operations due to the non-arrival of vital spares (recorded with some feeling in the subsequent report), the second line period ended on 26 August with the departure of *Cleveland* for Subic Bay. This allowed the ship to be

replenished, while the aircraft were undergoing a period of maintenance and repair. During the port visit the squadron also received news that the Cobra had been cleared to use the much more effective 5-inch Zuni rocket system. Modification work on the helicopters began immediately.

The Zuni is a weapon virtually unique to the USMC in the attack helicopter world. Almost twice the size of the familiar FFAR, the unguided Zuni is nearly 6 feet long, and carries a much larger warhead over considerably greater distances. This increase in range allowed the Cobra to engage anti-aircraft batteries at a much safer stand-off distance. The weapon was originally designed to be used from high performance fixed-wing aircraft, and owing to its size and weight the Cobra could only carry two rockets in each of the two LAU-10 four-shot pods. The squadron pilots found no difficulty in using the Zuni, and its extra punch made it very popular. It was somewhat less popular with the maintenance crews however, due to the airframe damage inflicted by the powerful rocket efflux.

After the completion of all the preparatory work, *Cleveland* moved out into the harbour while the ordnance, including the Zunis and their launch pods, was taken aboard. On 5 September the ship sailed for Hong Kong, where the entire company could enjoy a few days liberty before rejoining the war.

Arriving back on station on 13 September, the Cobras lost no time in firing their first Zunis, and by

27 September they had made the first night-time firings (which must have been a spectacular sight). Such was the secrecy surrounding the MARHUK missions, that HMA-169 would assert some years later that it was the first unit to carry the Zuni operationally, presumably being unaware of HMA-369's prior claim to that distinction.

Operations continued much as before during September and early October, with some diversion being provided on 16 September when one of the Cobras was involved in the rescue of two Air Force personnel whose F-4 had come down in the Gulf of Tonkin. Bad weather increasingly hampered operations, although the squadron often succeeded in flying through conditions that could, at best, be described as marginal. The third line period concluded with MARHUK 561 on 8 October, after which the ship left the area bound for Okinawa.

With the squadron disembarked at MCAS Futenma, there was time for briefings and familiarization flights to be given to several visiting staff officers, including Brig Gen Miller, who had arrived with no less than eight air medals for presentation to squadron personnel. During these formal ceremonies, the command of HMA-369 was passed to Maj D L Ross.

The following day (25 September) the unit's personnel and equipment were flown out to the ship on board CH-53 Sea Stallions of HMH-462, and late that afternoon seven newly painted AH-1Js arrived to

complete preparations for sailing the following morning. Arriving in the Hon La area at around 13.00 hours on 29 September, MARHUK 562 was in the air just 90 minutes later, to check what the enemy had been up to in the squadron's absence. A steady increase in activity was noted, and operations continued to be launched apace, despite disruption caused by the ever worsening weather, and the brief visit of a 'big mother' aircraft (a heavily armoured Sikorsky HH-3 operated by the US Navy's HC-7 combat SAR squadron), which occupied a large chunk of *Cleveland's* flight deck during its stay.

HMA-369 thought it was headed for home on 9 November. Maj Gen Brown (CG 1st MAW) paid a visit to the ship just as MARHUK 620 was recovered. The visit coincided with the general's birthday, and a considerable party was thrown in his honour. *Cleveland* had turned for Okinawa, and with most of the squadron's kit already stashed away, the men could be excused for thinking that they really 'had it cracked'. It was not to be. Orders were received to return to the anchorage at Hon La, and by the following day they were back on station.

At the end of November *Cleveland* finally returned to Subic Bay where the third and final change of ship was made. The squadron cross-decked to USS *Dubuque* (LPD-8), and offloaded one of the Cobras that had received combat damage during MARHUK 622. By the evening of 11 November they were back at Hon La.

The following day MARHUK 708 commenced operations by attacking floating supplies. The success of the earlier missions had, by September, made the use of all transfer craft virtually impossible, and supplies were simply being dumped over the side of merchant ships and left to float ashore. The weather continued to worsen, but by far the biggest storm clouds were gathering over the so-called 'peace talks' in Paris.

The last American ground troops had left Vietnam in August 1972, and the communists had continued

ABOVE
There are no known pictures of the Zuni rocket being fired during the MARHUK missions, but this shot of a test-firing from the AH-1W prototype gives some idea of the tremendous power of the weapon as it leaves the aircraft (Bell)

BELOW
The big Zuni rockets were carried on the outer weapons stations to minimize airframe damage when they were released (Mike Verier)

Standard load for day missions, MARHUK Operations

2 × Zuni (5″)
In four-shot pod
(LAU-10)

7 × 2.75″ WP
for target marking
(LAU-68)

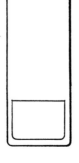

1200 lb
fuel

600 rounds
20 mm

7 × 2.75″ 17 lb
warhead (HE)
with VT fuse
(LAU-68)

2 × Zuni (5″)
in four-shot pod
(LAU-10)

their assault on the South while apparently talking about peace at the conference table. President Nixon was finally driven to take action by the obvious intransigence of the North's negotiators. On 18 December he ordered the talks to be suspended until 8 January, and simultaneously ordered the execution of 'Linebacker II'—the unrestricted bombing of North Vietnamese targets by US Air Force B-52s. Within ten days the North had had enough, and on 30 December they formally agreed to negotiate a truce.

By this time, following the recovery of MARHUK 759, USS *Dubuque* was on her way to Kao Hsiung and liberty, and Maj Ross was at last able to begin work on a detailed assessment of the achievements of the operation.

These achievements were considerable, and the Cobra gained much admiration throughout. Given that this was an entirely untypical mission, the major task faced by the squadron was the development of tactics for survival in an incredibly hostile area. It was quickly found that modification had to be made to the usual helicopter formations, in order to allow maximum cover by the wingman of his leader. The 'loose deuce' formation—more commonly associated with fixed-wing operations—was found to work well during daylight hours, but when the emphasis shifted towards nocturnal missions it became clear that the use of single aircraft would be more sensible.

This came about primarily because of the difficulties of controlling two aircraft at night, but it was also found to place less strain on the helicopters and on the crews. Initially two-hour patrols were tried, but flying at heights of between 50 feet and 500 feet with little or no visual reference, meant that the command pilot was on instruments throughout the mission, and this was much too fatiguing. Eventually a one-hour-on/one-hour-off routine was established, which had the dual benefit of giving the crews some rest, while needing less fuel—and therefore allowing more ordnance—per mission.

In this way the squadron was able to maintain aircraft on station continuously from 12.00 hours to 0.600 hours. Given that the LPD was not a specialized aviation vessel, the total number of night hours achieved was remarkable. A major influence on the tactics was the absolute requirement that aircraft were not to go 'feet dry' (over land) at any time, which did pose problems with the night illumination of targets. The Cobra has a flare capability (the SUU-44 Mk 45 system), but the rules of engagement effectively prevented it from being used. The alternatives were to call in fixed-wing aircraft or use naval gunfire, and the latter was more generally applied. The target area had been mapped and divided into predesignated sections labelled A to K. The pilot would simply call 'Shoot point Charlie', and get an immediate response with star-shells placed just where he needed them.

One of the difficulties of the MARHUK operation was the possibility of having to attack fleeing enemy targets while under fire from the shore. Although only used once, the cry 'Launch the hog' produced what was described as the 'awesome' sight of the standby Cobra (kept on hot-pad status on the mother ship) running along the shoreline to loose off 76 white phosphorous FFARs in one pass! This provided an excellent smoke-screen for the attack aircraft, as well as causing a considerable increase in the laundry bills of the recipients on the ground.

There is still much comment and opinion concerning the vulnerability of helicopters in battle, and the MARHUK missions shed some interesting light on the subject. The Cobras were operating in a very confined area which positively bristled with enemy weapons, including heavy calibre 57 mm, 37 mm and 23 mm guns, and the more numerous .51 calibre machine guns. Hits from any of the heavier weapons would certainly have been lethal to a light helicopter, but the Cobra's manoeuvrability and small cross-section made it a very difficult target for the opposing gunner. This is graphically illustrated by the fact that during more than six months of operation there were 140 recorded instances of hostile gunfire, and on only seven occasions were the aircraft hit. Only one of these (MARHUK 622) resulted in damage that could not be repaired on the LPD, and there were no aircrew injuries whatsoever.

A very important factor contributing to this level of safety was the doctrine of aggressive response. Any enemy position firing on the Cobras could expect to be engaged in return, either directly by the helicopter, or by fixed-wing strike, naval gunfire; or all three if the assets were available. This tended to make the AAA gunners nervous, and they fired in short, sporadic bursts which certainly increased the helicopter's chances of survival. The Cobras were also in markings that had been specifically 'toned down' for the operation. This supposedly rendered the task of the gunners even more difficult, and may have contributed to their low hit rate.

The Cobra was found to be a reliable weapons platform throughout the operation. The Zuni was particularly appreciated for the stand-off it provided, although before it arrived the squadron had been achieving surprisingly good results with 'lofting' techniques for the standard FFAR. The 20 mm M-197 turret gun was still a relatively new weapon in those days and suffered from a number of teething troubles—particularly gun jamming. The crews finally got on top of the problem and discovered, like most new systems, that 'the more you used it the better it stayed up'. The gun eventually achieved some impressive results, and was certainly feared by the enemy.

There were other, more technical, lessons learned. The operation of various night-vision devices proved disappointing, whilst photographic work using nothing more sophisticated than a hand-held 35 mm camera equipped with a 150 mm telephoto gave excellent results. Shipboard maintenance in less than ideal conditions highlighted a number of ingenious

and entirely practical solutions devised by the squadron, as well as generating valuable information to feed into the requirements for future attack helicopters. MARHUK may have been a 'one-off' operation, but it demonstrated dramatically the potential of the Cobra in a purely Marine environment.

Before the whole MARHUK experience reached its successful conclusion, the new projects team at Fort Worth had been busy proving the up-rated KingCobra, and exploring the possibilities for its export. The Iranian Government was eventually to order over 200 'standard' twin-engined Cobras, and the USMC agreed to lease one of its precious AH-1Js

Despite the suggestion that helicopters are vulnerable during combat operations, over 750 MARHUK missions were eventually flown without loss. A number of the aircraft involved in 1972, including this example currently serving with HMT-303 at Camp Pendleton, remain on the active list 17 years later (Mike Verier)

to serve as a pattern aircraft. The full implications of the Iranian deal will be discussed later, but the leasing arrangement was a smart move on the part of the Marines, because the development work done on the aircraft paved the way for the next step in Cobra evolution—the AH-1T.

Chapter 9
A longer, meaner Snake

The US Marine Corps was clearly delighted with the AH-1J. The overall capability of the aircraft had finally proved, even to the most sceptical of individuals, that the attack helicopter did have a place on the combined arms team. During its limited land-based combat in Vietnam the SeaCobra had demonstrated a remarkable versatility, and the success of the ship-borne MARHUK missions simply reinforced its reputation—particularly its ability to deal with coastal defences.

Feedback from the MARHUK operation was already being assessed by the Marines when they were invited to the KingCobra launch in September 1971. Bell had done a lot of work on potential improvements to the Cobra family, and both the Army and the Marine Corps were attracted by the possibility of more power, increased take-off weights, and perhaps above all, an effective anti-armour capability.

The Marines are in the business of initial assault—generally of a coastal area, although not exclusively so. This places the Cobra in the position of being the only heavy support available to the 'grunt' (infantryman), until the beachhead is secured and tanks and artillery are landed. Fixed-wing elements can give a degree of support, but the helicopter's response is often more immediate, and certainly more precise—telling points when your own soldiers are in close proximity to a potential target. An effective anti-armour missile would be able to remove 'surgically' most of the major threats to any invasion force.

The helicopter-launched version of the Hughes TOW missile was still in its infancy when the KingCobra programme was initiated, but the demonstration prototypes carried mock-up launchers, and the missile was one of the suggested updates for the Marines' AH-1Js. The missile's excellent performance during the April 1972 Easter Offensive in Vietnam had impressed everyone, and the subsequent ICAP programme to clear the Army's AH-1Gs to fire

TOW was watched with interest by the USMC. When it was finally decided to design an upgraded 'Marine' Cobra, TOW was incorporated into the specification.

The Iranians ordered AH-1Js in 1972, and their aircraft incorporated an uprated powerplant and transmission to produce a TOW compatible airframe. The same combination could have been retro-fitted into USMC Cobras, but the Marines were sure that an even more capable aircraft would be needed for the future. It was, therefore, decided to use the 'J International' as a starting point, and go on from there to produce a new generation of SeaCobras—an aircraft that would eventually be designated AH-1T. During the design process, an opportunity was also taken to iron out a lot of the in-service niggles with the AH-1J, things that were only really apparent after several years of operational experience. Most of these changes were nothing more than details, but Bell did take particular note of the complaint that it took two days of hard work to complete an engine change on the existing aircraft.

The maximum take-off weight of the AH-1T would be about 14,000 lb, compared with the AH-1J's 10,000 lb. More power was an obvious first requirement, and because the AH-1J was already transmission-limited, a new drive-train became essential. The power was provided by a Pratt & Whitney (Canada) T400-WV-402 'twin-pac', which was similar in most respects to the AH-1J's powerplant, but capable of delivering its full 1970 shp through the new transmission. The transmission itself was virtually identical to that used on the big Model 214 transport helicopter, and it was capable of handling all the potential power from the new engine, plus a degree of growth if necessary. To absorb the extra power, the AH-1T was fitted with a bigger, more advanced rotor. The disc-span was increased to 48 feet, and the chord of each blade went up from 27

TOP
This early US Army AH-1G was one of several painted in an Arctic high-visibility scheme, while supporting a military research effort in the area. At least one of the aircraft (69-16440) also acquired a quite splendid sharkmouth design. Note the absence of weapons, and the original (port side) mounting of the tail rotor (Bell)

ABOVE
This Cobra—military serial unknown—served as 'NASA-730' for trials with the PNVS nose turret. This AH-64 equipment was eventually adopted for 15 TH-1S 'surrogate' trainers. Known locally as 'Mother', the aircraft features a very discreet sharkmouth design
(NASA via Bryan Wilburn)

TOP

The last two production AH-1Js were taken off the assembly line before completion, and converted to a new AH-1T standard. This produced an altogether more capable helicopter, with more usable power and a bigger rotor. The first AH-1T was 59228, which flew for the first time on 20 May 1976. The second aircraft (59229) was more fully equipped, and carried the nose-mounted sighting system for TOW missiles (Bell)

ABOVE

The twin-engined AH-1J at last gave the US Marine Corps an aircraft that was more suited to ship-borne operations. It was corrosion-proofed, equipped with a better gun, naval communications and a rotor brake (Bell)

RIGHT

During its operational evaluation, the YAH-63 conducted a wide variety of weapons trials. This remarkable picture shows the moment of release for a full ripple-fired salvo of 2.75 inch FFARs. Note the trials cameras mounted on the lower horizontal tail and above both wing tips (Bell)

ABOVE
The full-scale mock-up of the YAH-63 was temporarily shown in this bizarre 'desert' camouflage scheme. Coloured rotors might look very smart in a brochure, but seen from above in flight they could advertise the aircraft's presence (Bell)

OPPOSITE ABOVE
South Korea was the only other customer for the 'J International'—an aircraft originally developed for Iran. Eight aircraft were delivered during 1978, all with the full TOW missile system. During 1986 a further order was (reportedly) placed for 21 examples of the latest AH-1S variant (Bell)

RIGHT
Seen here on the ramp at Camp Fuji, this AH-1S Cobra was one of two built at Bell's plant in Fort Worth, Texas, and shipped to Japan in June 1979 to serve as pattern aircraft for the production line which was eventually set up in 1983. With a Hughes TOW missile launcher mounted beneath the starboard stub wing and the magazine bay door open, Cobra 73401 belongs to the Air Training Support Squadron of the Japanese Ground Self-Defence Force, based at Akeno (Photo by Hideki Nagakubo)

OPPOSITE ABOVE
The AH-1T+ SuperCobra wore this striking black and gold paint scheme while it was being demonstrated during the mid-1980s. This was the first T700-powered Cobra, which was eventually developed into the AH-1W production version for the US Marines. It carries the full TOW missile system and the AN/ALE-39 chaff/flare dispenser (Bell)

LEFT
The four-bladed SuperCobra with the modified Model 680 rotor flew for the first time on 24 January 1989. Since that date, trials have shown that the new configuration lives up to all expectations (Bell)

ABOVE
Even before it had taken to the skies this particular Cobra had suffered from the recent redesignation of the many models which make up the formidable family of Bell attack helicopters. Starting life as an AH-1S, this Cobra, destined eventually for the US Army, is now an AH-1F! Although the single Avco Lycoming T53 turboshaft engine and the majority of the helicopter's sub-assemblies have been installed into the fuselage, the M197 20 mm rotary cannon and the ammunition magazine are conspicuous by their absence, as is the nose mounted M65 TOW laser sighting unit.

AH-1J (157769) was used extensively in support of the AH-1W programme. It was among the first Cobras to carry the Hellfire missile system, and its front (above) and rear (right) cockpits are both dominated by the Hellfire launch panel (Bell)

inches on the AH-1J, to 33 inches. The blades were of advanced construction, and featured swept tips to give some noise reduction. The new dynamics were significantly heavier than before, which gave a smoother ride and made the AH-1T an even better weapons platform than its predecessor.

The increased diameter of the rotor necessitated a longer tail-boom, and a larger, more powerful tail rotor. The vertical fin was truncated in the manner of the UH-1 series, and a ventral fin was added to maintain yaw stability. The tail-boom extension on the AH-1T is deeper and somewhat less elegant than the tail designed for the earlier KingCobra, which has resulted in the AH-1T being immediately recognizable by the characteristic double kink in the lower fuselage line. To maintain the aircraft's centre of gravity a 12 inch plug was inserted in the fuselage between the cockpit and the transmission housing. This had the effect of moving the entire cockpit section—including the front landing-gear cross-tube—forward, creating space for an additional 400 lb of fuel and a new avionics bay. The provision of longer undercarriage skids completed the structural changes.

As far as weapons capability was concerned the major change was the adoption of TOW, but even this was not fitted to all the AH-1Ts immediately: budgetary restrictions in the mid-1970s forced the Marines to accept a slow retro-fit programme for more than half the aircraft. The system included the nose-sight and TSU package, as well as the necessary wiring and 'black boxes' (which were sited in the tail-boom). Both crew members were also provided with the Sperry-Univac helmet-mounted sight, which could be slaved to the M-197 turret gun or nose-sight to ensure faster target acquisition. A new recoil compensator, developed to enable the Iranians to use the M-65 TSU with the M-197, made it possible to fire the AH-1T's gun accurately out to its maximum range without giving the gunner a vibration-induced black eye!

It was decided to use the last two AH-1J airframes as the 'prototypes' of the AH-1T. The first aircraft (59228) was taken off the production line and converted during 1975 and early 1976. It flew for the first time as a 'plain' AH-1T (i.e., not TOW-equipped) on 20 May 1976. The second aircraft (59229) was produced to full TOW standard, and flew some time later.

The AH-1T quickly proved itself to be an excellent aircraft, meeting or exceeding all NAVAIR performance requirements during the arduous testing phase of Navy Preliminary Evaluation (NPE). It was the first naval helicopter to run up against the stringent contractor guarantees laid down by NAVAIR, which formalized the difficult area of reliability and maintainability standards. The aircraft was required, for instance, to complete nine out of ten two-hour missions without any failure of mission-critical components. The effort Bell had put into correcting

squadron niggles really paid off here. During the trials, company and service pilots flew 24 such missions without significant failure, and during the period only three minor discrepancies occurred out of a 'permissible' total of eight. This fine record resulted in only 1.34 minutes of unscheduled maintenance time per flight-hour, giving an unprecedented man-hour/flight-hour ratio of 0.0225.

Production machines were coming off the Fort Worth assembly lines by mid-1977, and by May 1978 HMA-169 at Camp Pendleton received the first of 33 'standard' AH-1Ts ordered by the Marine Corps. Twenty-four TOW-equipped aircraft were ordered as follow-ons, and again HMA-169 was to accept the first operational example—this time on 26 January 1979. Students of US military serials may find some confusion with these totals, because 15 of the airframes were originally ordered as AH-1Js, but the batch was later converted to AH-1Ts.

During this period Bell made a paper proposal to the Iranians for a further updated machine, described as the AH-1T+. This aircraft was to incorporate all the modifications of the TOW-equipped AH-1T, but it would be powered by twin General Electric T700-GE-700 engines, driving the rotor and dynamics of the similarly-powered Model 214ST (which was originally to be manufactured in Iran). In the event, the collapse of the Shah's regime precluded this plan, but work on the AH-1T+ continued and it was subsequently flown and offered to the USMC as a logical improvement in capability.

Before looking at the AH-1T+ in any detail, we should perhaps pause to examine the AH-1T's service record. Like all its predecessors, the 'T' variant of the Cobra family has been involved in combat, and has been in widespread service as the Marine Corps' front-line attack helicopter. Indeed, the evident success of the aircraft has encouraged the Corps to seek extra resources to double its attack helicopter force. This will be achieved by a combination of remanufacturing older aircraft, as well as procuring new-build examples. In the meantime the AH-1T is doing the job.

The AH-1T in service

Capt John Peyton DeHart is a US Marine Corps pilot, whose wide knowledge of the Cobra family has been invaluable in the preparation of this service narrative. He graduated from flight school in 1981, and has flown the AH-1J, AH-1T and AH-1T(TOW). Having served in Grenada and Lebanon, he completed a stint as a flying instructor, and is currently flying the AH-1W. He is not the first to use the term 'sports car' to describe the Cobra, and he finds the aircraft responsive and pleasant, even 'fun' to fly. Like others he is aware of the limitations of the aircraft, but in common with generations of 'Snake drivers' he sees no reason for the aircraft not to complete any mission within its flight envelope.

LEFT
Powered by twin General Electric T700-GE-700 engines, the AH-1T+ was originally designed for the Iranians. Unfortunately, the downfall of the Shah ruined any possibility of another lucrative contract (Bell)

BELOW LEFT
The first AH-1T (59228—seen here quite late in its test programme) shows the big 48 foot diameter rotor, with swept tips and a broader chord than the original AH-1J. Note the AIM-9 Sidewinder missiles (Bell)

RIGHT
The AH-1T has a more powerful tail rotor and the vertical tail is also truncated at the top, bringing it closer aerodynamically to that of the UH-1 series (Mike Verier)

ABOVE
The telescopic sight unit (TSU) and M-197 gun could both be slaved to the Sperry-Univac helmet-mounted sighting system (HSS). The starboard-front radar warning receiver is visible aft of the sighting turret (Mike Verier)

BELOW
The 12 inch 'plug' between the cockpit and transmission-housing of the AH-1T allows space for more fuel and a new avionics bay (Mike Verier)

LEFT
Capt (then Lt) Peyton DeHart seen here off the coast of Lebanon in 1983. Note the 'tactical' bone-dome cover: this is quickly removable to show the reflective 'rescue' tape normally applied to all service helmets (via Mike Verier)

ABOVE
The 'Iwo Jima' class assault ship, USS Guam *(LPH-9), was used by HMM-261 as its base of operations during the Grenada and Beirut actions. These ships were specifically designed to operate helicopters, and normally accommodate a mixed group of AH-1Ts, UH-1Ns, CH-46s and CH-53s* (Capt Peyton DeHart, USMC)

BELOW LEFT
The Iranians ordered 202 TOW-capable AH-1Js in 1972 (Bell)

Grenada

That the Cobra was involved at all in the Grenada incursion had an element of chance about it, and the fact that two out of the four machines available were lost to enemy action was particularly tragic. The circumstances in which three very brave men lost their lives have never been completely reported before now, primarily because the military command in Grenada was reluctant to repeat the miserable Vietnam experience of total media freedom on the battlefield.

It should perhaps be understood that the US involvement in Grenada was not in any way an 'invasion'. Following a particularly bloody coup, during which the Prime Minister, Maurice Bishop, and members of his Government were brutally murdered, the newly-installed Cuban-backed revolutionary council began rounding up and imprisoning suspected sympathizers of the previous regime. This caused a great deal of concern throughout the Caribbean, culminating in a specially convened meeting of the Organization of Eastern Caribbean States (OECS) on Friday 21 October 1983. This meeting, which took place in Bridgetown, Barbados, considered what action should be taken.

All the member states agreed that the rightful government should be restored to power as quickly as possible, but lacking the military resources to enforce the decision, they appealed to Barbados, Jamaica and the United States for assistance. The urgent diplomatic approaches were agreed in principle by the three countries concerned, and a formal Request for Assistance was made under Article 8 of the OECS Charter on Sunday 23 October.

The American Government had been monitoring the situation on Grenada with growing concern. There were about 1000 US nationals on the island (mostly students at a medical school), and contingency plans for their evacuation were already being made. This kind of evacuation is a well-rehearsed routine, and while it clearly requires a military presence for both transportation and security, it does not normally seek to engage local forces. The urgency of the request from OECS meant that the Joint Chiefs of Staff now had to consider a full military option.

In the midst of a clearly deteriorating situation on the island, a letter was received at the White House from the Governor General, Sir Paul Scoons. He was the Queen's official representative on the island and although his position was largely ceremonial the Reagan administration chose to recognize him in the circumstances as representing legitimate authority. His plea for outside intervention and protection was therefore treated as an official request for help.

The order to execute what became known as

Operation 'Urgent Fury' was actually given on Saturday 22 October 1983, to a US Marine Corps task force that was already in transit for a routine deployment to Lebanon. Centred on the 'Iwo Jima' class amphibious assault ship, USS *Guam* (LPH-9), PHIBRON FOUR had embarked 1700 combat-ready Marines, their armoured vehicles, and the helicopters of HMM-261.

'D day' was set for Tuesday 25 October. Army, Marine and Ranger units would all be involved, but due to a lack of time and an anticipated shortage of fuel on the island, it was decided that the 82nd Airborne would initially have to operate with only its UH-60A Black Hawk transport helicopters; the supporting AH-IS Cobras would have to follow later. As a result of this decision, the four Marine AH-ITs embarked on USS *Guam* would be the only helicopter gunships available to take part in the initial assault.

The full details of the outcome of Operation 'Urgent Fury' are a matter of historical record. Suffice it to say that the US/Caribbean forces that liberated Grenada and restored democracy to its people, encountered remarkably heavy resistance from a well-armed and determined foe. Capt DeHart's after-action report covering the Cobra's involvement during the first two days of the incursion is reproduced below. As it was written at the time it stands as a tribute to a number of brave men who confronted the dangers of an island assault in the full knowledge that they would be part of a relatively

small task force, operating in an exposed environment without the normally anticipated level of support.

At 0440 25 October the first section of Cobras (30 Giguere/DeHart and 32 Howard/Seagle) took off USS *Guam*. The second section (33 Watson/Ryan and 31 Diehl/Gielow) took off for the pre-dawn assault. Approx 0530 the command was given to proceed to the zone. The first section dashed ahead to arrive two minutes prior to division of 46s. First section circled the LZ and relayed information on conditions and obstacles in the zone. As the first division approached the LZ, led by second section of Cobras, the first section flew north over a nearby runway to a hill that had been a suspect AAA site. A ZPU-4 opened up from the hill top. Acft 33 put a burst of 20 mm on the hill using NVG and the helmet sight subsystem, and aircraft 31 covered their pull-off with HE (2.75) and 20 mm. 30 and 32 set up an ordnance pattern and fired 2.75 inch HE rockets and WP rockets. Exact figure for 32 unknown. Would estimate seven 2.75 inch HE and 200 rounds of 20 mm. 30 fired 44 2.75 inch HE and WP. Ground units later found that the Cobras had silenced two ZPU-4s on that hill. Further action included orbiting overhead for zone security and visual recon of likely avenues of approach.

30 and 32 returned to USS *Guam* at 0625 for re-arm and re-fuel. Scharver replaced DeHart at that time. 30 and 32 launched at 0730 to relieve second section on station over Pearls Airport. Second section returned to USS *Guam*, re-armed, and performed recon of northern part of island. First and second sections provided eyes in the sky for

LEFT
The arrival of the US Army's AH-1S Cobras during the Grenada operation was held back by lack of fuel on the island, so the UH-60 and CH-46 transports had to be supported by just four USMC AH-1Ts (Sikorsky)

ABOVE
Aircraft No 33—'El Tigre'—over the palm-fringed beaches of Grenada during the Urgent Fury *operation in 1983. This aircraft survived the conflict, and was credited with at least two Soviet-made ZSU anti-aircraft weapon kills. Two aircraft, Nos 30 and 32, were lost in the action* (Capt Peyton DeHart, USMC)

ground FAC and ground commander, with recon north to end of island and south to Salinas Airport. In southern sector (where Army had landed), a target was identified by ground FAC. Acft 33 popped up for a hover TOW shot. A 90 mm recoilless rifle located in a house was destroyed in the first hit. A military vehicle, mounting a ZPU-4, was eliminated in the second hovering TOW shot.

At 1300 33 and 31 returned to USS *Guam* for refuel. DeHart replaced Gielow at that time. 30 and 32 flew south where Army units suggested possible targets. Approx 1330 acft 32 was hit by 23 mm rounds. Capt Howard, his right forearm blown off and right leg broken in three places lowered collective with his left arm and flew towards land. As the engines wound down he broadcast to Capt Seagle to take the acft. Capt Seagle was unconscious. Finding a clear space to land, Capt Howard input a large flare with the cyclic, crooked his left leg to hold the cyclic in position then raised collective with his left arm, finally lowering the nose with the cyclic for an upright landing. Capt Seagle woke up, got out and pulled Capt Howard out of the burning acft. Capt Seagle pulled Capt Howard a distance away from the acft. As small arms fire whizzed overhead, the fire began to cook off the 2.75 in rockets and the TOW missiles on the wing stubs. As Capt Seagle tried to move Capt Howard towards a safe treeline, Howard said he was dead anyway (due to blood loss) and for Seagle to leave him, to head for safety. When Capt Seagle refused, Capt Howard pulled out his pistol with the intention of shooting himself so that Seagle would be free to go. Seagle took the pistol away from Howard, put a tourniquet of radio cord wire on his forearm then moved off to the treeline.

All the while Capt Giguere/Lt Scharver in acft 30 were placing 20 mm and 2.75 in rocket fire on the AAA site and called in a Medevac. They stayed on the scene to ensure the safety of the downed crew and the Medevac helicopter inbound. When Capt Howard was picked up, Capt Seagle did not reappear from the treeline. Capt Seagle did not survive his wounds.

Acft 30 was hit by a different, nearby AAA a minute after the Medevac cleared the hostile area. An observer reported that the acft impacted water at an 80 degree nose-down attitude. Both pilots are missing. A destroyer steamed over the crash site and reported, 'Acft intact, no bodies in the pilot/co-pilot seats.'

Act 33 and 31 flew in the Delta pattern waiting for an on-call assignment. At 1610 they landed at Pearls Airfield for a possible mission that evening. An intelligence report of four APCs and a tank headed for the airfield caused them to launch at 1625. Both acft reconned the northern half of the island in search of the vehicles. They were not seen. At 1756 they left Pearls Airport and escorted Maj Gallagher's 46 that had developed problems back to the ship for a final shutdown of 1846.

Wednesday 26 October 83. Acft 33 (Watson/Ryan) and 31 (Diehl/DeHart), launched at 1345 to fly to Salinas Airport for a brief on a rescue operation. After receiving the brief on the assault the Cobras had two missions. 1. Protect the transports from suspected AAA sites, and 2. provide close-in fire support for the beach assault. The section launched at 1545 and escorted the transport helicopters to the LZ, continuing north towards the suspected AAA. Numerous passes convinced the pilots that there was no AAA threat at that particular location. As the section returned to the landing site acft 31 experienced a hydraulics failure and was returned to the secure airport. Acft 33 provided the CIFS by knocking out automatic weapons positions in a two-storey concrete bldg by firing seven TOW missiles and seven 2.75 inch HE rockets into the structure. The building and the weapons positions were totally destroyed. Acft 33 provided covering fire and escorted the transport helos back to the secure airport when the tactical extraction of troops and civilians was complete.

PREFACE

The citation reproduced here is for the posthumous award of the Navy Cross to Captain Jeb F. Seagle, United States Marine Corps Reserve, for action on 23 October 1983 on the Island of Grenada. Captain Seagle's award is the only Navy Cross that has been awarded for action since the close of U.S. involvement in the Vietnam War in 1973. The brave still serve.

Capt. Seagle's citation:
SEAGLE, JEB F.

For extraordinary heroism while serving as an AH-1T (TOW) Cobra Attack Helicopter Pilot with Marine Medium Helicopter Squadron 261, 22nd Marine Amphibious Unit conducting combat operations on the Island of Grenada on 25 October 1983. While conducting an armed reconnaissance mission in support of ground forces, Captain Seagle's aircraft was hit by multiple anti-aircraft artillery projectiles and forced down behind enemy lines. Having been knocked out by the blast, Captain Seagle regained consciousness after his fellow pilot had flown the aircraft to impact and found that his aircraft was on fire and burning out of control. As Captain Seagle exited the front cockpit of the Cobra, he saw that the other pilot had been critically wounded and remained helplessly trapped in the aircraft. With complete disregard for his own safety, Captain Seagle courageously returned to the aircraft which was now engulfed in flames and pulled him out. As unexpended ordnance began to cook off all around them, Captain Seagle carried the severely wounded pilot well clear of the danger. Now exposed to heavy enemy small arms and machinegun fire and faced with certain death or capture, Captain Seagle ignored the danger and remained to attend the wounds of the injured pilot by wrapping a tourniquet around his severely bleeding arm. Realizing that enemy soldiers were approaching, Captain Seagle fearlessly distracted them away from the helpless pilot and ultimately sacrificed his own life in an effort to buy time for the rescue helicopter to arrive. By his extraordinary courage, uncommon valor, and loyal devotion to duty in the face of danger, Captain Seagle ensured his brother-in-arms was rescued; thereby reflecting great credit upon himself and upholding the highest traditions of the Marine Corps and the United States Naval Service.

Lebanon

With its initial assault role fulfilled and the situation in Grenada under control, the US Marine task force resumed its passage to Lebanon. The environment in the Middle East was actually considered far more dangerous than the Caribbean area. The Cobras that were shot down over Grenada were lost in circumstances that the Marines would not normally have to face: the Corps' primary doctrine is that gunships will support heli-borne landings, and they in turn will have the support of fixed-wing elements and naval gunfire. In the Lebanon, as part of the Multi-National Force (MNF), their rules of engagement were once again highly restrictive, and yet they were likely to encounter advanced weaponry and electronic countermeasures, as well as 'ordinary' gunfire from the street fighting gangs and other heavily armed factions.

The AH-1T has many of the features found on the Army's AH-1S. The radar warning receiver is the same, and both aircraft are equipped with the AN/ALQ-144 electronic jammer. The AH-1T's twin-engined layout however, does not lend itself so readily to exhaust suppression, which makes it more vulnerable to IR-guided missiles. All USMC Cobras (including AH-1Js) are therefore fitted with AN/ALE-39 chaff/flare dispensers mounted in overwing pods. These can fire chaff rounds to break a radar lock, or flares designed to lure heat-seeking missiles away from the aircraft.

Owing to the USMC's more varied role, its Cobras are qualified to carry a wider range of weapons than the Army aircraft. The clearance of landing grounds for instance, necessitates the use of the huge CBU-55 store, which is an air-burst fuel/air explosive capable of flattening an area the size of a football pitch. Mention has already been made of the 5 inch Zuni rocket used by the Marines. This very effective weapon continues in service, although its use has caused some affront to the aerodynamics of the Cobra. Early firings of weapons such as the Zuni and the TOW, resulted in damage to the airframe, both from overpressure (which could peel the skin off the elevators), and from the powerful rocket efflux. The latter has resulted in the leading edge of the wing and the pylons having to be coated with an epoxy putty called 'Flexfram'—the idea being that this inelegant coating should burn off in preference to the skin of the aircraft.

Initially a symetrical weapons load was carried by the aircraft during operations over the Lebanon, with TOW on the outboard stations and rockets inboard. Experience of that configuration however, showed that firing the Zunis could at best melt the TOW wiring, and at worst 'cook off' an undemanded TOW round. The mix of armament was changed to overcome this problem, and the resulting imbalance amply demonstrates the AH-1T's flexibility—and indeed its weight-carrying capability compared with the MARHUK AH-1Js. The starboard outer pylon

ABOVE FAR LEFT
The official citation for Capt Seagle's posthumous Navy Cross

ABOVE
AN/ALE-39 chaff/flare dispensers—seen here mounted above the wing of a Sidewinder-equipped AH-1T during operations in the Gulf—have been a standard fitment on all mission-configured Marine Cobras for some years now. This is necessary because the twin-engined layout does not lend itself easily to exhaust suppression (US Navy)

retained the four-shot TOW launcher, while the inner carried a seven-shot pod of 2.75 inch FFARs with WP for target marking. On the port side were two four-shot Zuni pods, one loaded with point-detonating fuses, and the other with proximity fuses for air-to-air use.

Using the Zuni for air-to-air combat may sound a little strange, but pending the general issue of Sidewinders it was certainly better than nothing. An attacker has no way of knowing if the rocket smoking towards him is guided or not, but he must assume that it is and take evasive action. Proximity fusing does at least give a chance of damaging the attacker if the warhead explodes close to him, and in any event the Cobra has bought a little extra time which can be used to good effect.

When he was asked about AH-1T operations with

TOP
The CBU-55 fuel/air explosive is a cumbersome weapon, but it can flatten a huge area of trees and scrub to form an instant landing ground (Bell)

CENTRE
The sacrificial Flexfram putty protects the leading edge of all surfaces that are likely to be burnt by the Zuni's powerful efflux. Note the angled inner weapons pylon, and the empty chaff/flare dispenser (Mike Verier)

BOTTOM
The massive size of the Zuni rocket can be gauged from this picture of an experimental stores arrangement on an AH-1T. The aircraft is equipped with an AN/ALE-39 chaff/flare dispenser, an AIM-9 Sidewinder, a long-range fuel pod, and the four-shot LAU-10 Zuni pod (Bell)

the MNF, Capt DeHart transcribed some relevant pages from a diary he kept at the time, and again they are reproduced here unabridged. The entries reflect the boredom, frustration, excitement and amusement of military life, and they refer to a period of operations that began (for Capt DeHart) only three weeks after leaving Grenada. It is helpful to understand that only four weeks before these events occurred, nearly 250 Marines were killed in the suicide bombing of their temporary barracks in Beirut: hence the preoccupation with any kind of small boat approaching the US Navy assets in the area. The Cobras were operating from USS *Trenton* (LPD-14), which is the same class of ship used to launch the MARHUK missions off North Vietnam, and US *Guam* (LPH-9), the 'Iwo Jima' class flat-top assault ship that had brought the squadron into the area direct from Grenada. The diary entries are prefaced by a brief scene-setting note by Capt DeHart.

Employment of USMC Cobras in Grenada was standard enough. Off the coast of Beirut, during my particular cruise (policies varied on different cruises), we were held in ready reserve should the Marines at the airport need fire support. The other major mission was that of standby combat SAR (Search and Rescue). An F-14 would be sent over the city to take photos (a TARPS mission), and we would launch one CH-46E with two AH-1Ts to orbit just offshore in case the jet was knocked down. That never occurred.

Monday 21 Nov 8
aboard LPD-14, USS *Trenton*
Was awakened at 0200 by the sound of 'General Quarters, General Quarters. This is not a drill!' After a predictable mad scrambling about the room we got down to the aircraft to find Maj Outlaw and Capt Maisel strapped in (they had the gouge on not tying boots etc until later). This was the small boat threat alert though we didn't launch. Sat in the aircraft for 20 minutes then returned to the rack as the ship steamed away from the coast. At about 0330 someone came into the stateroom and told us to be on five minute alert. We again suited up and strapped into the aircraft. Probably had 15 minutes of consciousness then went to sleep. About 0530 was awakened and headed back to the rack for half an hour's sleep. Got up, ate, then flew a two hour formation hop. Later launched for some kind of combat SAR, but it was cancelled before we were briefed or started to fly it. Came back and went to sleep.

Tuesday 22 Nov 83
Woke at 0600, ate, briefed and took off for a formation hop. The day was clear and pretty. Figured Ryan to be a better stick but it was perhaps just a bad day (we are still somewhat shell-shocked from yesterday) tired-wise. Came back and as soon as we were relaxed in the debrief, 'Launch the alert Cobras!' We scrambled, a little smoother than last time and got down to the aircraft. Myself and Ed Umstead were in Dash 2 which had not been refuelled yet. No taking off with virtually no gas so we waited for a pump as Lead took off. By the time we were gassed the mission was cancelled (some of these missions are standby for a US plane making photo recon of the city. If he isn't shot down, the mission is cancelled), so we sat in the aircraft on the deck. After securing from standby we went back upstairs and almost

went to chow when, 'Launch the alert Cobras' over the 1MC. We scrambled and took off at noon for a rendezvous with a combat SAR CH-46; the mission was then cancelled. We returned to the LPD and sat in the wardroom waiting for the 1MC to tell us to go again. After three days we have a Pavlovian reaction to this alert, I can only imagine what five months will do to us. When the call to 'establish flight quarters' came over the speaker we, as one, jumped to our feet and were out of the door. The grunts watching the movie with us jumped back or sank in their chairs at the surprise of our co-ordinated quick mass exit. We got some night time in and landed on the LPH so the *Trenton* could go out to sea for a 'pump and dump'. I remained on alert 'til dawn's early light.

Sunday 4 Dec 83
About 0800 got into the aircraft for 5 minute alert status—getting smarter, brought a book with me. 0840 launched for a combat SAR mission. Shut down on the deck ten minutes later but remained seated in the aircraft until 1100 while (I believe) center forgot about us. Pretty dull stuff being strapped in that long without flying. 18 A-6s and 24 A-7s staged a strike in the Bakaa Valley against (I think) Syrian/Iranian missile sites. Lost one A-7 (pilot recovered), and one A-6 (one pilot taken POW other dead—or so we hear). We expected retaliation. At 2330 we were called on alert and launched as the airport had come under some form of attack 8 KIA 2 WIA not real sure of details. Darkest night I have ever flown in! Returned to the *Trenton* at 0130 and went to sleep (we had just orbited; *Trenton* didn't go into the beach).

Wednesday 7 Dec 83
Probably the most flying I've ever done in a single day—didn't mind it a bit (6.7 hours). Did some CAS FAC(A) missions with some A-6s (with mixed results), also fired some ordnance. Fired a Zuni, nothing much to it. Just a lot throatier than a 2.75 inch coming off the wing. Was called away to intercept a small craft in the vicinity of the LPH. Pretty big actually, 50 feet + but not hostile. Also stood by for a TARPS mission but it didn't go. Fell in formation with an F-14 (got inside his radius of turn); when he realized that he couldn't out-turn us he levelled out and did an aileron roll. Would have given a month's pay to do one with him in the Cobra! Oh well, maybe next generation helicopters will do that safely.

Thursday 8 Dec 83
Took off in the morning for a formation hop. Heard the airport was taking rounds so we called center and told them we were on station. They said: 'OK, hot pump, then shut down, we'll call you if we need you.' They never called.

Wednesday 14 Dec 83
The *New Jersey* fired her 16 inch guns today; I saw the flash from a distance. The guys on the beach said that the sound was so loud that they thought it was incoming not outgoing.

Wednesday 4 Jan 84
Flew as pilot in command for some flawless hops. Ran two sections at a practice target in the water. Did some 2 vs 1 on a Lynx and flew with the gas mask on.

Saturday 7 Jan 84
Took off in the morning and did some formation work with bounces on the *Trenton*. Did some air-to-air intercepts

during the second hop. Pretty fun stuff, a change of pace and helpful to the controllers too.

Sunday 8 Jan 84

. . . One Marine killed today as he stepped off a '46 at LZ Oriole (in front of the embassy). I just finished about eight landings in that zone when last I was in a Huey. Got to stay alert, I guess.

Monday 6 Feb 84

The situation ashore seems to have deteriorated. Smoke obscures the city and extends from the beach a mile (fires and explosions, cordite-caused). We are not being directly attacked but are getting a good amount of spillover. The entire city seems to have erupted in firefighting. We briefed 4 '46s and 4 Cobras for an evacuation operation (the civilians from the embassy). This really got my adrenalin going! I am ready to begin a new phase of our operation (it would also be exciting to be present for a successful evacuation operation—the conclusion of the Beirut operation). The evacuation most likely won't go tonight, but it sure is an option that could be executed. I hear an A-6 close air support mission didn't go well this evening. The RABFAC was intermittent and they had trouble acquiring the target. One bomber was 7000 m off target with one stick. A great sense of frustration on my part since General Joy already owns the assets that can surgically remove/destroy any target in the town. But he has forgotten, or doesn't know, that Cobras exist.

Tuesday 7 Feb 84

Today the weather cancelled most of our morning flights. The wind was gusting to 40 knots and the ship is pitching and rolling enough to slide chairs around the room. In the afternoon we rebrief the noncombatant evacuation operation of the US Embassy. Stood by all afternoon in the ready room as the *Guam* drove north of the city within four miles of the coast. That affords us some wind protection. Launched at 1620 and after arming almost immediately, got into a 180 degree out racetrack pattern. As we rolled in, I acquired the target with the TSU and tracked the area (target in this case meaning the LZ in front of the embassy). Three '46s shuttled in one time apiece and picked up everyone without a hitch. After the last one left, there were some artillery explosions nearby but they were of no consequence at that point. Returned to the *Guam*. By the end of flight operations we had removed the embassy personnel and some 200+ nonessential personnel from MAU HQ LZ. I believe the nonessential are support groups and Seabees-type Marines. This isn't a full scale evacuation yet.

Wednesday 8 Feb 84

The backload begins in earnest now. Have heard the President has ordered us out of our positions and back onto our ships. No doubt we will remain in our locations offshore or some form of MODLOC rather than sailing off for good. Got up in the afternoon and found the *Trenton* for the *Guam*

The Cobras were operating from USS Trenton *(LPD-14) and USS* Guam *(LPH-9), in the troubled waters immediately off Beirut. Note the guard manning a machine-gun to the left of the aircraft's tail (Capt Peyton DeHart, USMC)*

LEFT
A Cobra with FFAR pods turns into the mists of a Grenadian morning. Just visible on the back of the weapons pods are radiation (RADHAZ) shields. These are simple foam plastic discs covered in aluminium foil, which are taped across the back of the pods to prevent the ship's radar from inducing stray voltages in the ordnance firing circuits. Without these precautions, the power of a modern radar is enough to 'cook off' the rockets (Capt Richard Ryan, USMC)

BELOW
The 'Iowa' class battleship, USS New Jersey *(BB-62), was held just offshore throughout most of the American involvement in the MNF. Her 16 inch guns could loft a one ton shell right over the city of Beirut and into the Shoufe Mountains beyond. If the land-based Marines came under artillery attack,* Jersey's *response could be devastating* (USN)

(her electronics are down). Got in a flight of F-14s escorting two Russian patrol planes (Bears) out of the area. Held a reasonable cruise turn position for a minute or two then they were out of the area. Did formation work for the rest of the hop. The *New Jersey* has been firing all day. She is hitting Syrian positions to convince them to stay out of the intercity fight. We went to battle stations just as we sat down to evening dinner. Got the aircraft off in under four minutes (we had to pause to put on my flak vest); threat was a Syrian gunboat possibility.

Thursday 9 Feb 84
Woke up just before 0600 to the sound of General Quarters bells. Great confusion as we woke up and ran out to the aircraft. It was a preplanned evolution, don't know what the purpose was other than just a generally higher readiness posture. Flew formation in the morning. Afternoon hop did formation and checking of civilian shipping. Landing on the *Trenton* (the LPD has two helo spots on the aft deck), has been interesting in the last few days. Today I landed between a '46 on spot one and a Cobra on the back half of spot two. Winds were called from the port bow at forty knots. Good approach and well planted landing. What a great way to live!

Friday 10 Feb 84
Launched with the SAR bird in the morning. Flew in the local area north of Beirut abreast of Junea. Did formation work and listened up for any signal that the retrograde effort needed fire support. At various times, the effort is called 'permissive' with no threat due to some truces the General was able to work out. At other times the zones will be hot, but no calls for us yet. Hot pumped then checked out civilian shipping. Am very sorry that we Cobras aren't playing a more active role here. A mission of 'be on station we'll call if we need you' is preferable to 'do your own thing, we'll call if we can't do anything else'.

Sunday 12 Feb 84
Woken up at 0530 and told I was on the schedule. Had set my alarm for six, so I guess that was necessary just to keep me off balance. Packed after the brief and took off for a hop that included some formation, spotting a Russian AGI, and checking the area for other shipping. After the first hop I got out and we cycled some of the ordnance crew and mechanics into the front seat for a ride. It was a real treat for them and is a good motivator for guys that work so hard for the aircraft that they rarely (if ever), get a chance to fly in. I don't mind giving up some of my flight time for that purpose.

Saturday 18 Feb 84
While waiting on the flight deck of the *Trenton* for a ride back to the *Guam*, I watched as two Cobras came in for the break. God what a thrilling sight and sound! As they came roaring in from astern in parade formation they are one pretty sight. The throaty growl is all the more impressive.

The US Marines were disappointed that the 'surgical' accuracy of their TOW-equipped AH-1 T's was not used to the full in Lebanon. This example, with a full complement of missiles and a loaded chaff flare dispenser, remains shackled to the deck of USS Guam, while some of the less efficient assets were given combat tasks. Note the 'toned down' sharkmouth decoration (Capt Peyton DeHart, USMC)

Chapter 10
New engine: new era

Undoubtedly one of the most important aspects of any aircraft is its powerplant. The influence that this can have on the success or failure of a project cannot be overstated. Take for instance the marriage of the Rolls-Royce Merlin engine with the Spitfire, Hurricane and Mustang—all three of which played a significant part in the shaping of modern history. In the case of the Spitfire, development of the powerplant (culminating in the Griffon series) eventually resulted in late-model aircraft that could take off at double the weight of the first prototype, and yet still be capable of displaying a huge advantage in virtually every aspect of its performance.

The development during the mid-1970s of General Electric's T700 engine was to have a similar effect on helicopter evolution. As with the arrival of the first gas turbine powerplants for helicopters, this new-generation turboshaft promised greatly increased power, higher standards of reliability and much improved operating economics. The engine now powers a wide range of helicopters, including the H-60 Black Hawk/Sea Hawk series, and the AH-64 Apache. Total sales of the T700 have already topped 5500 units, and its power output has risen from the original 1550 shp to a potential 2700 shp.

After the long and costly development of the AAFSS proposal, its final cancellation once again deprived the US Army of a successor to the 'interim' Cobra. Bell had configured its KingCobra prototype as an AAFSS contender, and in the dying months of the programme the aircraft was flown in competition with Sikorsky's S-67 Blackhawk and the ailing AH-56 Cheyenne. The evaluation report concluded that none of the three helicopters then available— even in fully developed form—would meet the new Army requirements, and it was suggested that a 'clean sheet' approach would be much more profitable.

No one at Fort Worth was troubled by this decision. The design effort on the two KingCobras had

certainly not been wasted, and the company still had more experience of attack helicopter production than anyone else in the industry. This level of expertise, together with the lessons learned from the AAFSS programme (largely at no cost to Bell), would stand them in good stead when the Army finally decided what it wanted.

When a competition was announced to develop the concept of an Advanced Attack Helicopter (AAH), Bell responded with considerable confidence. Submissions were also received from Boeing-Vertol, Hughes Helicopters, Lockheed and Sikorsky, all of which recognized the potential value of the final contract, both in technological and financial terms. In June 1983 Bell was selected as one of the two finalists, and the company received funding to build two flying prototypes and a ground-test airframe of the Model 409, which was subsequently designated YAH-63 for its service trials. At the same time Hughes Helicopters was awarded a broadly similar contract covering its

Model 77, which later became the YAH-64. All five of the original contenders were required by the Army to use two General Electric T700 engines.

The YAH-63 incorporated a number of changes from what had gradually become accepted gunship practice. The most notable of these was the transposition of the pilot and gunner stations, which enabled the pilot to sit in the front where he would have the best possible view for NOE flying. This was made possible by the transition from direct to remote viewing devices and sensors for the gunner, who could now be seated behind the pilot without any loss of effectiveness.

The TOW-equipped mock-up of the Bell Model 409 shows how the gun was positioned above the sensor turret. The 409 saw the first appearance of the 'flat plate' canopy (Bell)

TOP
The crashworthy undercarriage of the YAH-63 could be adjusted on the ground to reduce the overall height of the aircraft. This made it easier to transport by air. The sole remaining prototype is now at Fort Rucker's splendid Museum (Mike Verier)

ABOVE
The engines of the YAH-63 were widely separated to prevent the migration of any combat damage. Note the

external drive shaft to the rear rotor, and the interesting 'end plate' tail arrangement (Mike Verier)

RIGHT
Although the YAH-63 was never a pretty aircraft, the eventual winner of the AAH competition seemed like a mechanical wart-hog by comparison. The first few production AH-64 Apaches were ordered at the end of 1981 (McDonnell Douglas Helicopters)

Rather less comprehensible was the repositioning of the gunner's optronics pod to a new site below that of the gun. The engineering reasons behind this change were sound enough: airframe damage and systems malfunctions caused by muzzle blast had been a nagging problem with the original Cobra layout—especially as the guns got bigger—and Bell sought to eliminate the trouble by moving 'delicate' sensors away from the major source of vibration (mast-mounted sights were not a viable alternative at that time). In practice however, the acquisition of a target with the new arrangement forced the pilot to expose even more of his aircraft to danger in order to achieve line-of-sight with the optical system. This was obviously a questionable tactic in any high threat environment.

A number of new features on the aircraft attracted much praise from experienced combat aircrew and servicing engineers. The storage of ammunition and fuel was arranged in such a way that even a direct hit in the ammunition bay would result in the explosion being directed out of the airframe, hopefully leaving the aircraft recoverable. The main rotor mast was easily adjustable to two positions, which enabled it to be lowered without disassembly to facilitate rapid air transport. This was helped by a 'kneeling' undercarriage, which further reduced the overall size of the aircraft. Unusually for Bell, the new helicopter was

fitted with a tricycle wheeled undercarriage. This simplified ground handling, but it was also capable of absorbing an impact velocity of 42 feet per second in the event of a forced landing. The strength of the system was amply demonstrated during the flight-test programme, when a very heavy emergency landing (not a 'crash' as some authorities would have it) was successfully achieved without even breaking the canopy glazing.

The survivability aspects of the design included widely separated engines, which ensured that any explosion in one could not easily affect the other. All vital parts of the airframe were armoured, with the transmission components invulnerable to hits from up to 12.7 mm, and tolerant of damage from larger calibres. Control-system redundancy was inbuilt, and the YAH-63 incorporated (again for the first time on a Bell design) the now familiar 'flat plate' canopy, which was much easier to maintain and replace, and reduced the problem of detection from 'glinting'. The whole crew area was heavily armoured, with both fixed and movable panels.

The company stuck with the familiar two-bladed rotor for the new helicopter. The aircraft did not need to perform any negative G aerobatics, and the system was well proven in terms of reliability and survivability. The rotor used was 51.5 feet in diameter, and each blade incorporated dual steel spars in its massive

The prototype T700-powered aircraft (161022), with modified exhaust arrangement, flew during 1980, and convincingly demonstrated the efficiency of the installation (Bell)

42.6 inch chord. The blades had already demonstrated tolerance of hits from 23 mm HE cannon rounds.

The required armament was specified by the Army in its original contract documentation, and was common to both competing AAH finalists. The Rockwell AGM-114A Hellfire tactical air-to-ground missile was the primary weapon, and 2.75 inch FFARs were secondary: a turreted 30 mm cannon was installed in the extreme nose of the Bell design.

The YAH-63 was not an aesthetically appealing aircraft. Although it was never officially named, its somewhat portly appearance led to it being dubbed the 'Bell Whale' by Army pilots who saw it during testing. Ultimately it was the arguably even less attractive AH-64 Apache that won the AAH contract, and in December 1976 the Bell Model 409 programme was finally cancelled. The company did not pursue the issue, but neither was it going to waste all that development effort—especially the flight-testing of a highly satisfactory engine. Plans were being made to continue work with the T700, and the marketing people already had a customer in mind.

Less than a month after the cessation of work on the YAH-63, the company produced a brochure proposing that the Iranians build or retro-fit Cobras to a configuration then described as 'T+'. This was seen as an entirely logical development of existing production agreements. With US technical and financial aid, the Iranian Government was in the process of establishing a 'local' helicopter industry. The T700 engine and transmission package was being qualified on a stretched Huey derivative known as the Model 214ST. This aircraft was specifically intended for production by the Iranians, who would be ideally placed to sell its 'hot and high' capabilities throughout the Middle East. The AH-1T+ proposal combined the 214ST's engine and transmission, with some of the features from both the USMC's new (at the time) AH-1T, and the existing Iranian AH-1J. Fitted with a new composite rotor, the resulting aircraft would have delivered 75 per cent more power than the standard AH-1J, and at the same time offered a 25 per cent decrease in overall fuel consumption.

When the Shah's downfall put and end to these plans, the company had enough faith in the project to want to continue its development—albeit at a much lower level. On the basis of investigating the feasibility of upgrading the AH-1T, Bell was able to lease an airframe from the US Marines in December 1979, and this was flown shortly afterwards with the new engines. During the course of 1980, the T700-powered aircraft (161022) demonstrated both the power and economy of the installation convincingly, and the company was soon confident enough to let it participate in weapons-release trials. The whole programme was given a fairly low priority, because the Marines made no secret of the fact that they would like to get hold of some AH-64s, and were not particularly anxious to overplay the potential of a developed Cobra.

This attitude changed completely in 1981, when Congress refused to allocate any funds for a Marine Apache. As the result of this disappointment, and after considerable pressure from the Marines themselves, Bell was given a $4.1 million contract to complete the qualification of the GE T700-GE-401 powerpack for use on the AH-1T. The contract was awarded on 26 June 1983, Congress having already given approval for another 'attrition' batch of 44 new-build aircraft.

'SuperCobra'

The persistent shortage of helicopters in the US Marine Corps led to the formation of a number of 'composite' squadrons, operating a mix of AH-1T, AH-1J and UH-1 aircraft, rather than being dedicated to a single type. HMA-169 and HMA-369, both located at MCAS Camp Pendleton, California, and HMA-269 from MCAS New River, North Carolina, were all subsequently redesignated HM(L)As, while

HMA-773 continued to operate as a Reserve unit from NAS Atlanta, Georgia, using only AH-1Js.

The funding of the 44 new AH-1Ts was approved essentially to relieve the pressure on these composite units, and the order was described as fulfilling a requirement for additional/attrition-replacement aircraft. The re-engined 'AH-1T+' programme had been conducted quietly through its initial development period, and Congress was now pursuaded that the state-of-the-art T700 could have a number of positive benefits for the Marines, including a significant reduction of fuel costs and a marked improvement in overall performance. After acceptance of the T700 argument, the incorporation of other improvements and updates in the new batch of aircraft were agreed with relatively little fuss.

The development airframe gradually acquired extra avionics, grew cheek bulges, and sprouted exhaust suppressors. During trials it carried Sidewinders, Hellfire, TOW and a gamut of other ordnance, as well as being fitted with a wide range of operational features, including an AN/ALQ-144 IR-countermeasures set and the AN/ALE-139 chaff/flare dispenser. Carrying the standard USMC dark green camouflage and low-visibility markings, the aircraft was externally unremarkable apart from the words 'SuperCobra' painted on the side of each engine casing.

After the announcement that full development funds were being made available, Bell's marketing

ABOVE
The T700 development aircraft is seen here carrying eight Hellfire missiles (Bell)

RIGHT
This pleasing study shows a TOW-equipped AH-1W over some desert testing grounds before its delivery to Camp Pendleton (Bell)

people slipped into top gear and 161022 was repainted in gloss black, with a striking gold snake running virtually the entire length of the fuselage: even the helmets used by the demonstration pilots carried the same image-building motif. At that time the aircraft was still being referred to as the AH-1T+, but when the first production machine was rolled out at Fort Worth on 27 March 1986, the Marines finally conceded that all the improvements justified the use of a new designation—AH-1W.

The present plans for the AH-1W involve not just the 44 new aircraft, but a progressive update of the existing AH-1Ts. As the new-build aircraft reach the squadrons they will be 'exchanged' for AH-1Ts, which will then be returned to Bell for modification to AH-1W standard. When the whole programme is finished, the active duty fleet will consist solely of AH-1Ws, and only students of serial numbers will be able to tell the difference between old and new machines.

The surviving AH-1Js cannot be brought up to full

AH-1W standard, but they will be modified to carry AIM-9 Sidewinder and eventually Hellfire missiles. As the AH-1W comes into service, the older 'J's will be progressively reduced to Reserve status. At the time of writing, the nominal organization of Marine units envisages six 12-aircraft active-duty squadrons and one Reserve, but this is bound to change. Funds for another batch of 34 new-build AH-1Ws were appropriated in the FY 1988 budget, and in the longer term the Marines would like to double their attack helicopter force.

AH-1W described

The airframe and major transmission components of the AH-1T have been used almost unchanged as the basis of the AH-1W. The powerplant housings had to be redesigned to accommodate the T700s, and while this was being done Bell took the opportunity to improve significantly their maintenance accessibility. As a result, the engines are now virtually 'podded', and have large access doors which double as work platforms—a valuable asset when the helicopters are operating from confined spaces on board ship. Both engines can be removed with minimal disconnections, and the time needed for a complete powerplant change is now measured in hours rather than days.

The -401 version of GE's T700 turboshaft is approximately 95 per cent common to the T700

powerplant used on the US Army's UH-60 Black Hawk. The navalized engine—which also powers the SH-60 Sea Hawk—has about 12 per cent more available power, and greatly improved corrosion resistance to cope with the salt-laden atmosphere encountered during maritime operations. The T700 series have long been regarded as among the most reliable helicopter engines available, and their MTBF (mean time between failure) figures have consistently beaten the military requirement by a considerable margin.

All the earlier Cobras had the electronics for the TOW missile system sited in the tail boom. This was originally done to solve a centre-of-gravity problem, but it clearly led to unnecessarily long and heavy cable runs. The revised engine installation on the AH-1W resulted in an aft migration of the CG, and this enabled all the TOW components to be moved forward, giving rise to the new, bulged cheek contours in the area of the ammunition bay. Access to the ammunition box itself (which retains the full 750 rounds capacity) is now from the starboard side of the aircraft.

The AH-1T rotor system has not been changed in any significant respect for the AH-1W, mainly because the USMC lacked the funds to develop and qualify a composite substitute. Proponents of the AH-64 have often seized on this as an operational limitation, citing the phenomenon of 'mast-bumping' as a fundamental weakness of the two-bladed

teetering rotor. Certainly the Cobra is limited by its rotor to positive G manoeuvres, but countless aircrews have lived with this so-called 'problem' for many years, and they still remain supremely confident of the aircraft's overall capabilities.

Bell, ever willing to provide a 'bespoke Cobra' service, would be more than happy to provide a different rotor system if the requirement ever arose, and low-key research into various multi-bladed or composite-material options continues, as will be discussed later. The current design team, however, is quick to point out that the existing arrangement gives the AH-1W a performance that comes remarkably close to that of the Apache, despite the fact that the Cobra is much cheaper, weighs less and has a smaller silhouette. It also has, they believe, a much more versatile armament package than the McDonnell Douglas product.

For the first time in an operational attack helicopter, the AH-1W has been provided with a dual primary armament system. The aircraft retains all the weapons available to the AH-1T (including TOW), but it has the additional option of using Rockwell AGM-114A Hellfire air-to-ground missiles. The AIM-9 Sidewinder has also been included, to give the aircraft a much-needed air-to-air capability.

Hellfire is a more recent weapon than TOW, and is generally considered to be the most accurate and lethal air-to-ground system currently available. The basic missile homes on reflected energy from a target 'illuminated' by a pulse-coded laser designator. The AH-1W is not yet fitted with its own laser, so all target designation will initially be from remote sources such as ground troops or USMC OV-10, A-6 and F/A-18 aircraft. This situation will change in the mid-1990s, when all the Hellfire-capable Cobras are due to be fitted with a stabilized FLIR sensor combined with an in-built laser designator.

The original proposal to use only remote target-designators for the USMC's Hellfire system, has certain advantages for the helicopter crews. With a simple 'pop-up' manoeuvre, the missile can be launched and on its way to the target, leaving the aircraft free to return to its 'hide' among the trees while somebody else provides the final targeting information. This is a definite advance on the wire-guided TOW, which needs a continuous line-of-sight to the target throughout its engagement, making the launch helicopter vulnerable to enemy counterfire for precious seconds during a long-range attack. The remote designator system also allows multiple engagements, with each missile seeking its own uniquely coded laser pulse. This can achieve a strike-

The armoured steel firewall between the engine bays can be seen in this view of an AH-1W under construction. The removable fuselage panels provide a high degree of accessibility (Bell)

US Army AH-1Es
taking off from
Howard AFB,
Panama in 1988
(Robert F Dorr)

ABOVE
The T700 engine is a remarkably small unit, and is well provided with access doors for front-line maintenance (Mike Verier)

RIGHT
An 'artist's concept' of the McDonnell Douglas/Bell solution to the Army complex LHX requirement (McDonnell Douglas Helicopters)

rate that would be impossible with TOW, but it requires excellent communications between the participants, and a separate designator for each target.

The major disadvantage of remote designation is that it transfers the targeting initiative away from the helicopter crew, which reduces the chance of a successful strike against highly mobile targets of opportunity. The need to call on the help of a designator will delay the action, and may even allow the target to escape. Certainly for the time being TOW will be retained, both as a cheaper alternative to Hellfire, and as a means of attacking those transitory targets that might have been missed by the two-element team. As Hellfire becomes relatively less expensive, and particularly as all the AH-IWs are equipped with a self-contained designator, the continued use of TOW might lose its appeal.

Hellfire first entered service in 1985 (on the US Army's AH-64s) and is still under active development. A number of companies are currently working on designs for an imaging infra-red (IIR) seeker to give the missile a 'fire and forget' capability, and an active-radar guided version has also been proposed. Some work has also been done on a passive radar-homing variant, which would seek out the emissions from hostile SAM or AAA sites. The future of this particular version however, now seems uncertain, since both the US Army and Marine Corps have qualified their helicopters to carry the much cheaper AGM-122 Sidearm missile. Sidearm is a derivative of the Sidewinder AIM-9 air-to-air weapon, and the AGM-122 programme involves the modification of

obsolete AIM-9C rounds with a passive seeker to home on SAM-type radars.

The AH-1W is undoubtedly the high-water mark of present Cobra development. Its increased capabilities, coupled with the proven longevity of the basic airframe, will assure the 'Snake' a place in front-line squadrons beyond the 1990s and possibly well into the next century. With LHX technology on the immediate horizon, it seemed unlikely that the Cobra would undergo any further significant changes, apart from the possible provision of a composite rotor. As readers will have learned, however, the Snake has been presumed dead more than once before.

Chapter 11
Snake Travels

The US Army and Marine Corps have obviously accounted for most AH-1 production, but the aircraft has also been very successful on the export market, and probably still represents one of the high points of combat helicopter development. Given the chance, foreign buyers would virtually queue up to acquire Cobras, although political and economic considerations will always be the controlling influences on future sales. The number of overseas air arms operating the type, however, continues to grow.

The earliest attempt to sell the aircraft overseas came during N209J's European Tour of 1967. In general, the European military would have welcomed a machine like the AH-1, but few individual air arms could afford to buy them in useful numbers. The British Army carried out a remarkably detailed evaluation of the prototype during a two-day stopover at Middle Wallop. Apart from the technical aspects of the aircraft, the final report closely examined the impact that the Cobra would have on Army logistics and training. It also noted, with some justification, that the kind of diving attacks from altitude employed in Vietnam, would be of little value in the high-threat environment of a European battlefield. In any event, the British Ministry of Defence decided not to buy the Cobra, and Bell continued to look elsewhere for overseas sales.

Curiously enough, the first export sale of Cobra was to the non-NATO Spanish Navy, who probably had less actual need for the aircraft than almost any other subsequent operator. The *Arma Aérea de la Armada* received four AH-1Gs in September 1972, and a second batch of four in January 1973. The Cobras were all assigned to *Escuadrilla* 007, and were intended to provide support for the Marines and (initially at least) the Spanish Navy's fast patrol boats. Within the first year, accidents had reduced the number of aircraft in service to five, but no replacements were ever purchased. At one time the

Navy expressed an interest in the twin-engined AH-1J, and the Spanish Army's aviation branch (*Ehjrcito de Tierra*) wanted the single-engined aircraft to meet its anti-tank requirement and actually conducted some evaluation flights. Political considerations then entered the arena, and the naval requirement was dropped in favour of an eventual fixed-wing element of AV-8As, and the Army contract went to the European-built Bo.105. The remaining Spanish Cobras soldiered on until 1985, when they were finally retired and reduced to the status of instructional airframes.

Australia and New Zealand were both considered to be likely sales prospects for the Cobra. As joint members of the ANZUS pact, both countries were directly involved in the Vietnam war, and both were already operating the Huey transport helicopter. A Bell sales team, led by 'Bud' Orpen, borrowed a predelivery AH-1G from the US Army, and conducted a demonstration tour of the area, in company with a Model-206 Jet Ranger. After a thorough evaluation of the aircraft, the Australian Government ordered an initial batch of 11 Cobras in December 1970. The military procurement process in Canberra was noted for its vacillation at that time, and the order was cancelled in October 1971. The borrowed demonstration Cobra (15662) was airlifted out of Australia immediately after its evaluation, and sent directly to a combat unit in Vietnam.

The Israelis probably received their first Cobras during the early 1970s, although the secrecy surrounding Tel Aviv's military procurement is so tight that information is sparse and unconfirmed. News film from the Middle East has certainly shown the

The Spanish Navy AH-1Gs were assigned to Escuadrilla 007. *After 12 years of service, some were retired and used for instruction, whilst the surviving leased airframes were returned to the US Army* (Bell)

machines in combat (particularly against PLO positions in Lebanon), but just how extensive these operations have been is open to speculation. It seems certain that the Israelis are happy with the aircraft, because arrangements were recently completed for the lease of an additional batch of 24 AH-1S variants. This deal is understood to be on a 'no-cost' basis, in exchange for the IAI Kfir fighters supplied to the Americans for dissimilar air combat training. The best information so far available indicates that Israel has received 12 AH-1Gs, 18 AH-1Qs and 16 AH-1Ss. It seems reasonable to suppose that most of the earlier aircraft have now been updated to the latest standards.

By far the biggest export programme ever undertaken by Bell, was the sale of AH-1Js and Model 214A transport helicopters to the Shah of Iran. As far as the Cobra was concerned, this order was to have far-reaching effects, because it led directly to the development of the AH-1W variant. The contract was finally signed on 21 December 1972, after two years of negotiations and demonstrations involving both governments and BHC. The order was for 202 modified AH-1Js and 287 of the advanced Huey-derived Model 214: the total value of the contract was estimated at $704 million.

The 'Iranian J' (also referred to as the 'J International') owed a great deal to the Model 309 KingCobra, and incorporated many of the features developed during that programme. The major improvements on the basic AH-1J included an uprated (1970 shp) T-400-CP-400 twin-pack engine; a stronger transmission derived from the Model-211 HueyTug; a nodalized gunner's seat to reduce vibration; an improved oil cooling system; SLAE avionics; an improved turret incorporating a recoil compensator; and a stabilized pantograph sight.

Later aircraft were to adopt the M-65 TOW sighting system, which led to further work on recoil compensation to enable the sight to operate at the full

ABOVE LEFT
*Seen here equipped with the XM-28 turret, the full TOW
sighting and launch system, and a pair of 2.75 inch FFAR
pods, this early Israeli AH-1S retains the old-style canopy*
(via Aldo Zanfi)

LEFT
*Later Israeli AH-1S models were fitted with the 'flat plate'
canopy and M-197 gun system. Note here the upturned
exhaust, and the censor's obliteration of the unit markings
on the tail* (via Aldo Zanfi)

ABOVE
*The AH-1Js for the Iranian Army were specially equipped
for operation in a hot climate, and incorporated an uprated
engine and transmission* (Bell)

*The first batch of
South Korean aircraft
were built to full
AH-1J International
standard, incorporating
the TOW missile
system* (Bell)

range of the M-197 gun. The results of this effort were incorporated in the AH-1T some years later. A bailed AH-1J was utilized by Bell as the pattern aircraft for the 'J International' prototype, and the initial test programme was conducted at the Patuxent River Naval Air Station, Maryland. Production deliveries to Iran were scheduled to begin in April 1974.

The overall contract with the Shah was ultimately intended to go much further than the supply of ready-made helicopters and their logistic support. The second phase of the programme would have resulted in the creation of a production capacity for helicopters in Iran, leading eventually to an indigenous design capability and a wholly Iranian-owned helicopter industry. The first product of this industry was to have been the Bell Model 214ST, which was already involved in its qualification trials when the Shah's regime collapsed. It was from this project, with its twin T700 engines, that the original AH-1T+ proposal emerged.

Currently cut off from all spares and technical support, it is widely supposed that few of the Iranian AH-1Js remain in a flyable condition. Certainly some of them are still around, because newsreel footage of the Iran/Iraq war has shown them in action as recently as 1986. How many there are, and just how long they can be kept going by an endless cannibaliz-ation process, is anyone's guess.

The only other user of the full 'J International' is South Korea, which received eight TOW-equipped aircraft in 1978. Most of these are believed to be still in service. During August 1986, the Koreans signed a $128 million contract with Bell for 21 examples of the latest AH-1S variant. The first deliveries from this batch were made during the summer of 1988.

The AH-1J is now out of production, and most of the current export effort is concentrated on the AH-1S. The biggest single overseas customer for this variant so far is Japan, which is in the process of building 62 aircraft under licence. The procurement of these is going ahead, but annual funding is limited and the whole programme will take some years to complete. The two initial aircraft supplied by Bell were 'production S' configured, lacking the exhaust-suppression kit and a number of other items of equipment. Subsequent locally-produced airframes appear to be fully up to US Army standards.

The Pakistan Army Aviation Corps ordered 22 AH-1S Cobras, which were delivered in two batches during 1984 and 1986. The first squadron was declared operational in March 1985.

LEFT, AND ABOVE, OVERLEAF
The first Cobras for the Pakistan Army were delivered in 1984, and became fully operational in March 1985. They were equipped with the exhaust-emission suppressor, but the IR-jammer was not fitted at this stage (Bell via Mike Verier)

A Jordanian AF AH-1S leaves Fort Worth at the start of its long journey to the Middle East. These aircraft have the K-747 blades, and are very close to US Army standard. The national insignia is not applied until the aircraft is formally handed over (Mike Verier)

ABOVE
Export Cobras such as this were supplied as equivalent to the US Army's AH-1S(MC) standard. In 1988 this designation was changed to AH-1F: this is an administrative change only, the aircraft is the same (Mike Verier)

The Turkish Army's air arm (*Turk Kara Kuvvetleri*) has had a long-standing requirement for anti-tank helicopters, and as a big UH-1 operator, the Cobra would seem the obvious choice. A sale of the AH-1S, complete with its TOW armament, was approved by the US Congress in 1983, but no orders have been officially confirmed at the time of writing. As Turkey is an important member of NATO, it seems unlikely that any political objection could have been raised in the meantime, which would suggest that the order—variously reported to be for between six and 26 aircraft—has been held up by financial constraints.

The Royal Jordanian AF has received 24 AH-1S Cobras, and these are now operational with No 10 and No 12 Sqns, based at King Abdullah AB. During the early 1980s the Egyptian AF is believed to have ordered 24 AH-1S Cobras as part of its 'westernization' process, but these were never delivered and the order has presumably lapsed by now. A similar problem appears to have blighted an order from the Greek Army air arm (*Elliniki Aeroporia Stratou*). During 1985, US Congressional approval was granted for a Greek purchase of 20 AH-1S aircraft and 1097 TOW rounds, but financial difficulties restricted the actual order to only eight Cobras—and even those appear to have been shelved in 1987.

The latest news of export Cobras is that the Royal Thai Army has been allocated $40 million for the purchase of an initial batch of four aircraft, together with their associated weapons and a logistics support base. Deliveries are slated for 1989/90, and if this order goes through, the Cobra will return to SE Asian skies just 25 years after the prototype was developed to combat 'guerilla' activity in the area. A neat turn of the wheel if ever there was one.

Epilogue...
or just another chapter?

In the three years spent researching this book, the Cobra programme, like any high-technology programme has evolved and changed, leaving a number of loose ends to be gathered together to bring the story up to date.

With the possible exception of a few instructional airframes, all the original AH-1G models have now been retired or updated to a later standard. Most of these continue to serve with front-line operational units, but as more AH 64 Apaches are delivered to the US Army, many Cobras are being released to National Guard contingents.

The Army has now attempted to make some sense of the wide variety of AH-1S mod-states, by giving them new designations: the ECAS or 'Upgun' AH-1S is now known as the AH-1E and the AH-1S(MC) as the AH-1F. The return to suffixes from the beginning of the alphabet was presumably done because the Marine Corps' AH-1W had used the last available suffix letter, and it now raises the interesting possibility of a 'Mk 2' AH-1G if any further modifications are carried out.

Despite the slow run-down in the front-line Cobra force, the US Army will still employ the aircraft in significant numbers well into the next century. Many of them are due to receive the long-awaited 'C-Nite' FLIR addition to the M-65 sighting system, which will enhance their capabilities further. A number of other improvements could also be in the pipeline. Far from being obsolete, the AH-1F continues in production as the primary export model as well.

The Hellfire-capable AH-1W is now in full operational service with the USMC, and the crews are delighted with it. The last of the original batch of 44 has been delivered, and Bell is now working on a second. The new contract, valued at $146.9 million, includes 30 firm orders and four options. In addition, 39 AH-1Ts will be converted to AH-1W standard.

All the original AH-1G airframes have now been retired or updated to a later standard (Museum of Army Flying via Mike Verier)

TOP
*A number of AH-1Js remain in service with the USMC,
but only in training and reserve roles* (Mike Verier)

ABOVE
*Early trials with a FLIR/laser-designator turret produced
this upturned nose profile, which was necessary to maintain
full gun elevation* (Bell)

BEWARE OF JET BLAST AND ROTORS

The two batches of new-build aircraft have virtually doubled the Marine attack-helicopter force, and allowed much-needed new squadrons to be established.

A significant number of the original AH-1Js remain operational with the Marines. There are no plans to withdraw these in the foreseeable future, because they continue to fulfil useful training and reserve roles. All aspiring USMC attack helicopter pilots are trained on the AH-1Js (and later the AH-1Ws) of HMT-303 at Camp Pendleton. The aircraft retain their full weapons capability, and would be a formidable back-up in any emergency.

The Marines have certainly been the most active US users of AH-1s since the end of the Vietnam War. Following their operations in Grenada and Lebanon, Cobras have been deployed to the Gulf as part of the multi-national convoy protection during the Iran/Iraq conflict. Initially this was carried out by AH-1Ts but the task was later passed to the more capable AH-1W, when HMLA-169—the first squadron to receive the type—was deployed there in early 1988. Operational missions were normally flown with FFAR pods on both inboard pylons, a Sidewinder on the starboard outer, and a four-shot TOW launcher on the other side; the 20 mm gun was armed at all times, and the aircraft were equipped with the IR-jammer and two fully-charged chaff/flare dispensers.

Bell and the USMC are aware that even the AH-1W could be improved, but allocation of funds is a constant problem. One of the most important requirements is a FLIR laser-designator; which would give the aircraft a true day/night attack capability, and enable the Hellfire missile to be exploited to its full potential. A system was developed by Texas Instruments during the mid-1980s, and its test programme on an AH-1T was very successful. The cost, however, was considered to be prohibitive, and an alternative was sought.

Under the auspices of the US Navy, the Israel Aircraft Industries subsidiary Tamam has now received a $70 million contract to develop a lightweight, stabilized FLIR/laser designator for the AH-1W. The Israeli Government is sharing the cost of the programme, and some elements of the system will be incorporated in the Israeli Cobras. The system is likely to be mounted in a ball-turret slightly bigger than the existing M-65 telescopic sight unit, which may result in a 'turned-up' nose profile if full gun elevation is to be maintained.

Serious consideration is being given to the possibility of reversing the traditional gunner and pilot stations. This would be an expensive option and is therefore unlikely to happen, but it was a highly

The USMC AH-1Ts were active in the Gulf during the Iran/Iraq war, mainly to provide a ship protection force (US Navy)

ABOVE LEFT
The FLIR trials were conducted on this converted AH-1T. Although the technical results were very good, the cost of the equipment was considered too high (Bell)

LEFT
Nap of Earth (NOE) flying over terrain such as this is becoming increasingly important to successful helicopter operations. Putting the pilot in the front seat now seems more logical than ever, but conversion of existing aircraft would be an expensive option. This is the first production AH-1W for the US Marines, seen here carrying TOW and Hellfire missiles, FFARs, the M-197 gun and AN/ALE-39 chaff/flare pods (Bell)

ABOVE
The Model 680 rotor was flown first on this Bell 222 corporate helicopter (Bell)

praised feature of the, unsuccessful, YAH-63, and it does have considerable merit now that NOE flying is so important.

One improvement to the Marine aircraft that does seem likely is the acquisition of the Air Data System fitted to Army Cobras which has made a significant improvement to the accuracy of weapons delivery. The sensor system itself is relatively inexpensive, but integrating it into the existing avionics and weapons systems might present more of a problem.

The application of a new four-bladed rotor to the AH-1W could be a long-term possibility—especially if the McDonnell Douglas/Bell proposal is selected to meet the US Army's LHX requirement. The all-composite Model 680 rotor has already done over 1000 hours flying on a specially instrumented Bell 222 corporate helicopter, and its smooth ride and control responses have impressed everyone.

The blades on the new rotor are carried on cleverly profiled composite yoke assemblies, which provide torsional flexibility to allow the blade-pitch to be changed without the use of bearings. This bearingless approach reduces all the complex machining operations needed to manufacture and maintain a conventional rotor, and gives it a virtually infinite life, with only a quarter of the number of parts of a normal hinge and bearing assembly.

After flying the 680 rotor on Bell's demonstration aircraft, the Marines were pleased with its remarkable manoeuvrability and lack of vibration. It was always understood that the Corps could not put any funds into the project, but it did renew the loan of the last AH-1T production aircraft—161022—for trials. This machine had already been used as the prototype for the AH-1T+, the 'SuperCobra' and the AH-1W programmes and flew for the first time fitted with a development Model 680 rotor on 24 January 1989 from Bell's Arlington flight research centre.

Currently known as the 4BW (four-bladed 'Whiskey'), the modified aircraft has four 25 inch chord surfaces in place of the two 33 inch blades on the original teetering rotor. The composite materials used are virtually transparent to radar, and the whole rotor assembly will have the ability to withstand direct hits from HEI rounds of up to 23 mm. The new rotor has already encouraged Bell to increase the AH-1W's gross weight to 16,300 lb, and its speed and G tolerance will improve markedly as the test programme gets into its stride. As a result of the increased speeds available, the horizontal tail of the 'prototype' has been moved aft by about five feet, and provided with large end-plate fins, similar to those employed on the Bell 222, for improved directional stability. Extra wing-tip weapons stations will also be fitted before the aircraft is handed over to the USMC for its operational evaluation.

A variant of the new rotor has already been selected by the McDonnell Douglas/Bell 'SuperTeam' for its submission to the $33 billion LHX contest. If the aircraft is selected, and the rotor goes into production on the massive scale necessary (more than 2000 LHXs are planned), the USMC could well be offered a very

attractive retrofit programme to bring all the current AH-1W aircraft up to '4BW' standard. Such an aircraft would be a formidable beast, with full night/adverse-weather attack avionics, TOW and Hellfire capability, and self-protection and anti-radar missiles. The idea of giving the 4BW a new name has already been mooted, with *CobraShark* and *Viper* among the possibilities.

Nearly a quarter of a century after its introduction as an 'interim' type, the Cobra is once more about to shed its skin and emerge as a bigger, stronger kind of snake. The aircraft is going to be around for many years to come, the final chapter in this story is a long way from being written. Meanwhile, a comment made by Gen Robert R Williams, the Director of Army Aviation when the Cobra was just coming into service, sums up a lot of feelings about the aircraft. He was asked about the naming of the Cobra, and he said: 'The big controversy was not naming the aircraft Cobra—it was with the Air Force over designating it the AH-1. The Air Force objected that the 'A' denoted an *offensive* weapon system. Our position was that we damn well *meant* it to be offensive. . . .'

ABOVE
The underside of the experimental Model 222's new rotor-head, showing details of the swash-plate and pitch-links. The mechanical simplicity of the bearingless system provides a virtually infinite blade life and vibration levels that are described as 'mostly below the level of human perception' (Bell)

RIGHT
The composite yoke assemblies provide the torsional flexibility for changes in blade-pitch (Bell)

MODEL 680

ADVANCED MULTIBLADED BEARINGLESS ROTOR

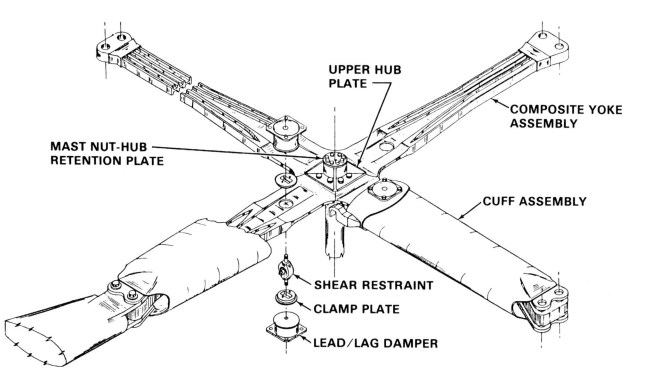

UPPER HUB PLATE

COMPOSITE YOKE ASSEMBLY

MAST NUT-HUB RETENTION PLATE

CUFF ASSEMBLY

SHEAR RESTRAINT

CLAMP PLATE

LEAD/LAG DAMPER

Appendices

Appendix 1
Evolution

For the first time in any publication dealing with the Cobra we have compiled, with the full co-operation of Bell Helicopter, an evolutionary diagram (Fig 1) that shows the relationship between the Cobra and other parallel programmes. It shows, again for the first time, the crucial part that the two KingCobras played in the evolution of the later variants and how even projects that were ultimately to lead into *culs de sac* had some influence on Cobra design.

Fig 2 shows the progression from the original 'G' models through the different 'S' variants to the aircraft as currently equipped and operated. The original intention to bring all surviving airframes to a common—AH-1S(MC)—standard was never re-alized and the Army was left with assorted aircraft in various mod-states, all with the basic AH-1S designation. To end this confusion they carried out an exercise in redesignation in 1988. As the H-1 series had run out of suffix letters, they decided to regress, thus totally confusing many people, including some eminent authors who have claimed that Bell delivered a number of AH-1Es. They didn't, of course, AH-1E being the new designation for the ECAS, Upgun 'S'. The only change in designation to affect Bell is that to AH-1F. Even the Army are having some problems; Fort Bragg has some old ECAS Cobras which are now designated AH-1E, but on the side of the aircraft the data panel giving the serial, procurement year and identity still says AH-1S!

Fig 3 shows the various stages of development and the several designations or acronyms by which they have been known, and includes the 1988 relettering.

Appendix 2
Weaponry and Equipment

Figs 4 and 5 illustrate the differences in weaponry between Army and Marine Cobras because of their different uses for the Snake.

The Army's weapon mix has changed little from that on the original AH-1G, the most significant addition being TOW. Fig 4 is reproduced, with their kind permission, straight from the manual, and shows the currently authorized permutations of stores.

The Marines, on the other hand, have always utilized a wider range of weapons and it was their requirement for 'droppable', as opposed to merely 'jettisonable', stores such as CBUs and retarded bombs that led to the canted inboard pylons found on USMC 'J', 'T' and 'W' Cobras. This wide range of weaponry and the later models' ability to load virtually any combination of stores, even asymmetrically, would take several pages to show in detail, so in Fig 5 I have simply shown the various stores compatible with each station and a 'mix' to give some idea of the 'W' variant's capabilities (it is to date the only attack helicopter able to carry TOW and Hellfire together). All the stores shown have been qualified; there are many more—such as Stinger—which are still in development and which it would be premature to claim as part of any aircraft's weapons suite.

Fig 4. The current range of weapons authorized for the AH-1F. Earlier 'G' models did not have provision for TOW but were otherwise identical, save that some airframes were equipped for the XM-35 20 mm cannon which was carried on station 2 only. Models up to and including early 'S' configuration also differed in having the M-28A3 turret with provision for 7.62 mm miniguns and/or M-129 genade launchers in any combination.

Fig 5 shows the remarkable range of ordnance

Fig 1

Cobra Evolution

Production models are shown in bold

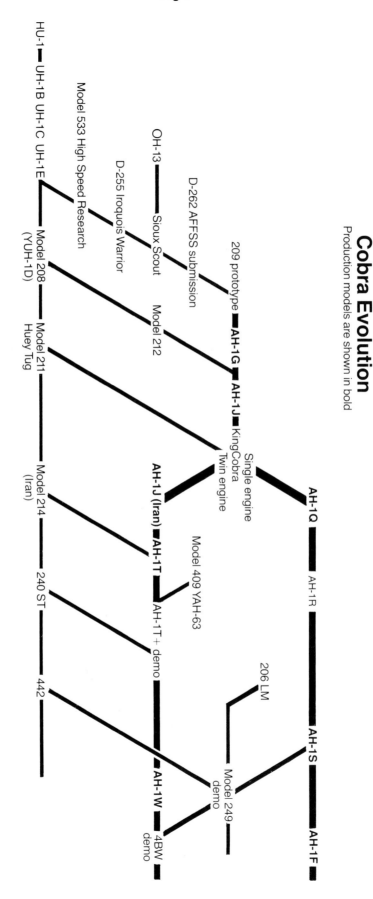

Fig 2

Evolution of 'F' from 'G' summary

	AH-1G	AH-1Q	Improved S* YAH-1S YAH-1R†	Production S	Upgun S	AH-1S (MC)
Designation	AH-1G	AH-1Q	Improved S* / YAH-1S / YAH-1R†	Production S	Upgun S	AH-1S (MC)
Acronym		ICAP	ICAM		ECAS	
1988 Designation			AH-1S	AH-1P	AH-1E	AH-1F
Engine	1400 shp		1800 shp			
Transmission	1134 shp		1290 shp			
Rotor	S40				K-747	
Armament	M-28 turret				Universal turret M-197 gun	
Sights	Pantograph	M-65 sight/tow helmet sights		Flat plate canopy		
				NOE cockpit RWR		IR exhaust ALQ-144 Radar Jammer Air data system Head-up display Laser tracker C-nite
Gross weight	9500 lb		10,000 lb			
Empty Weight	5809 lb		6300 lb	6278 lb	6419 lb	(min) 6598 lb

*Also known as 'Modified S'
†Sole R did not have TOW or helmet sights

Fig 3

Summary of designations and production

Bell model	Service designation	1988 redesignation	Notes	First Flight
209	N209J		First prototype	1965
	UH-1H		Briefly redesignated AH-1G pre-production, Two aircraft	1966
	AH-1G		Basic production version. 1127 produced including 38 for USMC and 8 for Spain	1966
	Z-14		Spanish designation for 'G' model	—
	TH-1G		Army designation for some aircraft used for training	—
	JAH-1G		One aircraft (71-20985) used in Hellfire trials	
	AH-1J		Twin engine version of USMC. 69 produced. Last two airframes (159228 and 159229) converted to 'T' and 'T' (TOW) respectively	1969
	AH-1J (Iran)		Improved version. 202 produced for Iran and 8 for South Korea	1974
	AH-1Q		(ICAP) 92 modified 'G's	1974
	YAH-1R		(ICAM) One aircraft (70-15936) modified 'G'	1975
	YAH-1S		(ICAM) One aircraft (70-16019) modified 'Q'. (See also model 249)	1975
	AH-1S (improved)	AH-1S	378 (including all 'Q's) modified	1976
	AH-1S (production)	AH-1P	Flat plate canopy. 100 produced	1977
	AH-1S	AH-1E	(ECAS) Also 'Upgun'. 98 produced	1978
	AH-1S (MC)	AH-1F	Cumulative results of above improvements to single-engine variants in production for US Army and export	1978
	TH-1S		15 produced from early 'S' airframes with Apache PNVS nose	1985
	TAH-1S	TAH-1F	Army designation for some aircraft used for training	
	AH-1T		57 produced for USMC, sometimes referred to as 'improved SeaCobra'	1976
	AH-1T (TOW)		Used to differentiate TOW equipped airframes. Dropped once all retrofitted	1976
	AH-1T+		Last production 'T' airframe (161022) converted to T-700 demonstrator. Designation also used for brochure proposal to Iran	1979
	AH-1W		Fully developed 'T'+. In production	1986
	4BW		161022 further modified to demonstrate four blade (680) rotor	1988
			Note. At the time of writing all surviving 'G' models in the army inventory have been reworked to S/E/F standard. During 1989 surviving 'T' airframes will be reworked to 'W' standard. In both cases, new and rebuild airframes will be distinguishable only by their serial numbers	
309			Two Kingcobra prototypes	1971
409	YAH-63		Three prototypes AAH contender	1976
249			Formerly YAH-1S airframe (70-16019) also Cobra II, PAH-II and ARTI demonstrator. Still in use	1979

carried by twin-engine Cobras and (right) the *service* model on which each system first saw qualification. Many items (eg ALE-39 chaff/flare dispenser) have been retrofitted to all variants. Note that TOW is applicable only to M-65 (turret sight) equipped airframes, and Hellfire is not (at present) included in the 'J' model's armament suite, although qualification was done using a 'J' model. Where Sidewinder is indicated Stinger may eventually be substituted.

Fig 6. The AH-1J airframe as currently flown. It is little changed from the original save for the addition of the ALQ-144 mount and the new anti-collision light aft of the rotor mast. AH-1Js now fly regularly with the ALE-39 overwing chaff/flare dispenser (see also the AH-1W in Fig 8).

Fig 7 shows aspects of the AH-1T and the AH-1T (TOW), including external and cockpit layout and the structural and equipment modifications and improvements from the AH-1J.

Fig 8 shows the AH-1W, the current production model for the USMC. This is the fully developed AH-1T +, and all surviving 'T' airframes are being reworked to this standard.

Fig 9. The author's conjectural diagram of the 4BW, based on information published by Bell. The demonstration model will feature the four-bladed, bearingless 680 rotor, a new laser/FLIR ball turret, overwing Sidewinder rails and a rebated tailplane with end-plate fins. The gunner and pilot stations may also be reversed.

The AH-1F is the current production model for the US Army and for export. Figs 10 and 11 show its external and cockpit layouts and comparison with Figs 7 and 8 will illustrate the divergence between the two production families.

The table in Fig 12 gives comparative data for size, weight, speed and powerplants for the various Cobra models and other types.

Appendix 3
Cobra Colours

As the reader will have seen from the illustrations, the Cobra has sported many colour schemes during its period of development and operational service. There is insufficient space here to deal with too many specific examples, but in the bibliography a number of publications are listed for those who need more details. In deference, however, to the amount of assistance I have received from members of the International Plastic Modellers' Society, I felt it important that some general notes and details, particularly of multicolour camouflage schemes, should at least be mentioned.

The notation used for colours is keyed to an invaluable US Government publication known as *Federal Standard 595A*. This document gives colour chips of hundreds of standard shades used by all government agencies, including the military. Each colour is identified by a four-digit code number, prefixed by 1 (for gloss finish), 2 (semi-gloss) or 3 (lustreless, or matt). FS595A is available for purchase by the public, and is therefore a readily accessible reference. More to the point, manufacturers quote FS595A numbers, so the colour given is the actual colour used, and not a visual approximation using another system. I am indebted to the Paint Shop at Bell for the very detailed assistance provided.

US Army

All the early AH-1G models were delivered in an overall finish of Olive drab 34087 (now renumbered 54088). Some had matt black anti-glare panels forward of the windscreen, and all carried the title UNITED STATES ARMY on the tail boom, and the aircraft serial on the fin: the lettering in both cases was six inches high, again in matt black. Cockpit interiors were Dark gull grey 36231, and the interiors of cowlings and access panels were a chromate colour approximating to 23793. This situation continued throughout the Vietnam period, although the NETT unit did experiment briefly with multicolour schemes. Resprays at a US Air Force facility were often traded for Army C-rations—delicacies that were not normally available to the 'blue suit' painters. Officialdom, however, frowned on the trading and the colour schemes, and both were short lived as a result.

During the early 1970s, the Army carried out a great deal of experimental work on possible camouflage schemes for both aircraft and ground vehicles. As well as the actual design of various schemes, research was conducted into the ability of a surface finish to absorb, rather than reflect, radar energy. An officer at Fort Hood is also reputed to have had his car painted in 'anti radar' colours. It looked horrible, but at least it enabled him to confuse police speed traps! The result of all this work was a scheme called 'pattern painting', in which the Army boffins worked out an exact pattern for every vehicle and aircraft in service. These consisted of four-colour designs, applied on a sort of 'painting-by-numbers' basis. The idea behind it all was that changing one or two colours, rather than the whole scheme, would enable climatic and terrain variations to be incorporated more readily. These paints were an early attempt at stealth technology, and are said to have worked so well that pilots occasionally baited Austin Approach by switching off their transponders and disappearing from radar screens.

As can be seen from Fig 13 (which is taken straight from the manual), the drawings provided to field units were rudimentary, and some variation in the finished article was to be expected. Essentially, the two main colours each covered 45 per cent of the subject, and the other two—one of which was generally black— covered the other 10 per cent between them. The table

Fig 4

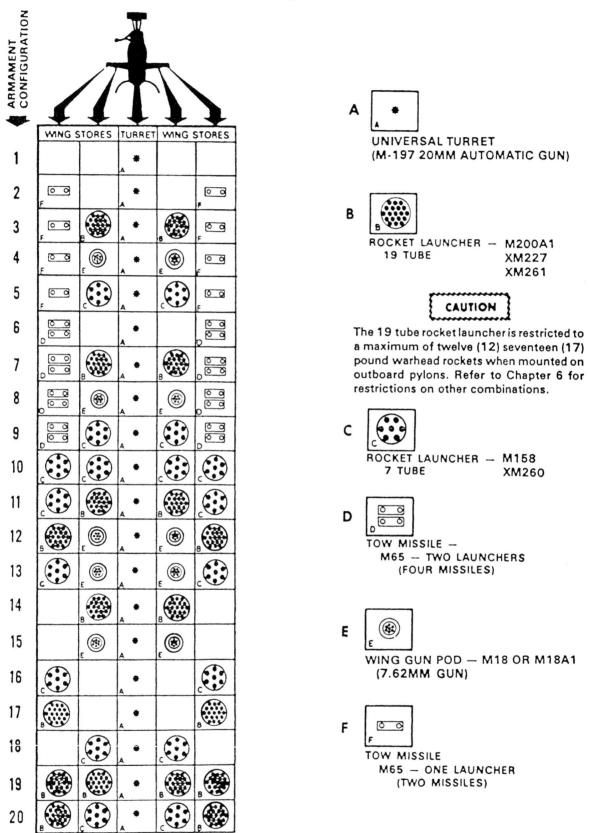

Authorized Armament Configuration

Fig 5

TWIN COBRA
ORDNANCE DEVELOPMENT

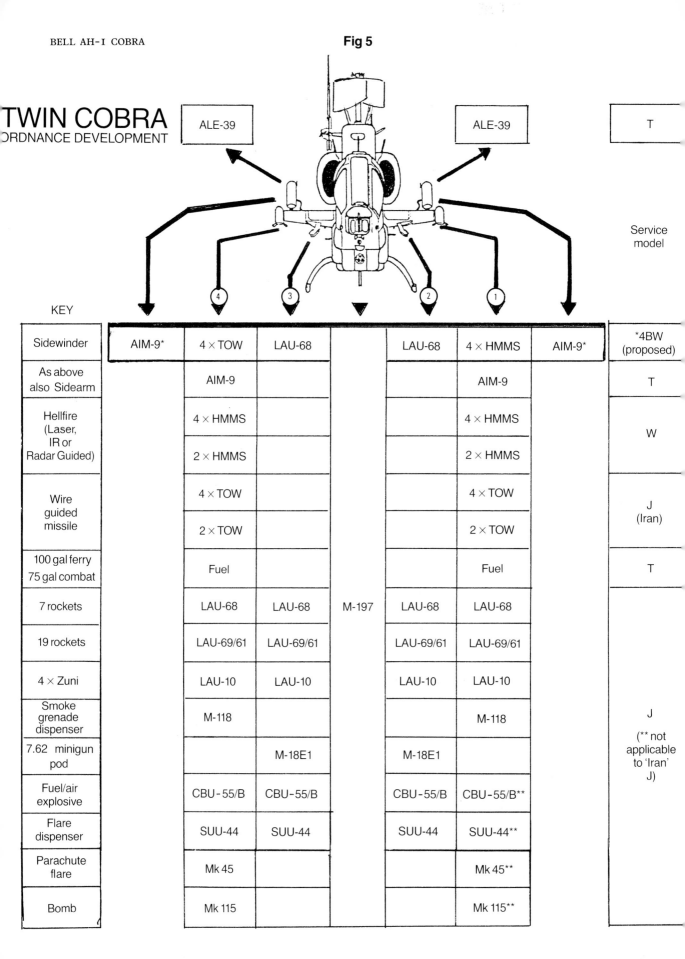

KEY	AIM-9*	4 × TOW	LAU-68	M-197	LAU-68	4 × HMMS	AIM-9*	*4BW (proposed)
Sidewinder		4 × TOW	LAU-68		LAU-68	4 × HMMS		T
As above also Sidearm		AIM-9				AIM-9		T
Hellfire (Laser, IR or Radar Guided)		4 × HMMS				4 × HMMS		W
		2 × HMMS				2 × HMMS		
Wire guided missile		4 × TOW				4 × TOW		J (Iran)
		2 × TOW				2 × TOW		
100 gal ferry 75 gal combat		Fuel				Fuel		T
7 rockets		LAU-68	LAU-68	M-197	LAU-68	LAU-68		
19 rockets		LAU-69/61	LAU-69/61		LAU-69/61	LAU-69/61		
4 × Zuni		LAU-10	LAU-10		LAU-10	LAU-10		
Smoke grenade dispenser		M-118				M-118		J
7.62 minigun pod			M-18E1		M-18E1			(** not applicable to 'Iran' J)
Fuel/air explosive		CBU-55/B	CBU-55/B		CBU-55/B	CBU-55/B**		
Flare dispenser		SUU-44	SUU-44		SUU-44	SUU-44**		
Parachute flare		Mk 45				Mk 45**		
Bomb		Mk 115				Mk 115**		

Service model

Fig 6

below gives the colours, their approximate FS595A equivalents, and their intended use.

COLOUR	ABBREVIATION	FS595 REF
White	W	37875
Desert sand	DS	30277
Earth yellow	EY	30257
Earth red	ER	30117
Earth brown	EB	30099
Field drab	FD	30118
Olive drab	OD	34087
Light green	LG	34151
Dark green	DG	34102
Forest green	FG	34079
Black	BL	37038

COLOUR DISTRIBUTION

	45%	45%	5%	5%
CONDITION	COLOUR NUMBER			
Winter US and Europe – Verdant (1)	FG	FD	S(3)	BL
Snow – temperate w/trees and shrubs (2)	FG	W	S(3)	BL
Snow – temperate w/open terrain (2)	W	FD	S(3)	BL
Summer US and Europe – verdant (1)	FG	LG	S(3)	BL
Tropics – verdant	FG	DG	LG(3)	BL
Gray desert	S	FD	EY(3)	BL
Red desert	ER	EY	S(3)	BL
Winter arctic	W	W	W	W

NOTES

(1) Verdant means generally green – in summer due to trees, shrubs and grass; in winter due to evergreens.

(2) This colour combination is for use only in areas that occasionally have snow which does not completely cover the terrain.

(3) This 5 per cent colour should be the camouflage shade that matches most closely the colour of the soil in the local area. A typical colour for such use is Sand, but Earth Red, Earth Yellow, or one of the others may be closer to the predominant soil colour and, in that case, should be used.

Although widely used on ground equipment, pattern-painting on aircraft was a rather specialized job, and it eventually proved impractical. Currently, therefore, all US Army Cobras are painted in a very matt (the finish is almost like fine sandpaper) dark green, known as Mil-C-46168 'Aircraft green'. The nearest FS595A equivalent is 34031, although the colour can be perceived as anything from dark olive green to nearly black depending on light conditions. In keeping with the low visibility doctrine, cockpit interiors and all external markings are black. Army aircraft on field service *do not* carry national insignia.

The US Army finish is also standard on AH-1S models supplied to the Pakistan Army and Japan, and

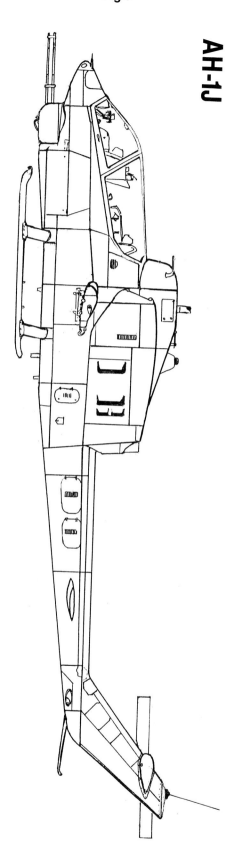

AH-1J

Fig 7

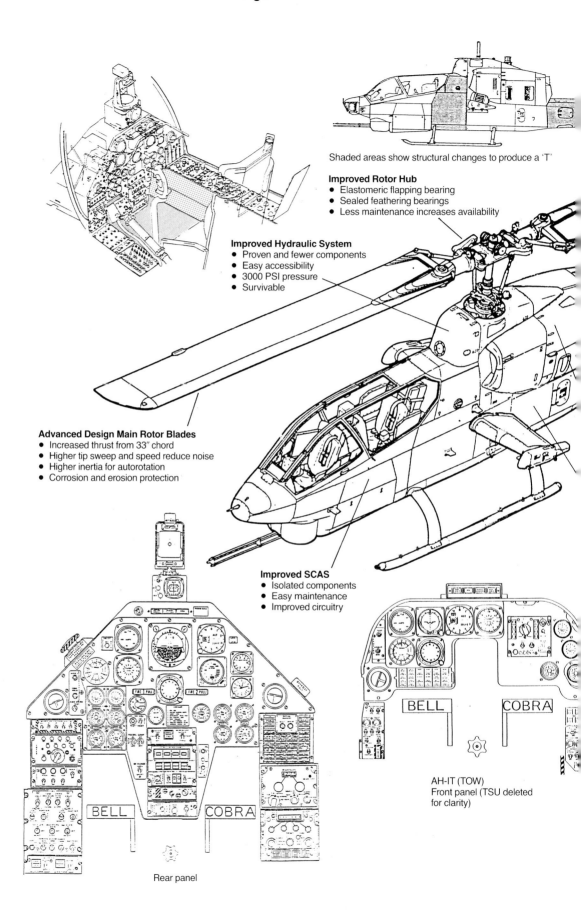

Shaded areas show structural changes to produce a 'T'

Improved Rotor Hub
- Elastomeric flapping bearing
- Sealed feathering bearings
- Less maintenance increases availability

Improved Hydraulic System
- Proven and fewer components
- Easy accessibility
- 3000 PSI pressure
- Survivable

Advanced Design Main Rotor Blades
- Increased thrust from 33″ chord
- Higher tip sweep and speed reduce noise
- Higher inertia for autorotation
- Corrosion and erosion protection

Improved SCAS
- Isolated components
- Easy maintenance
- Improved circuitry

BELL COBRA

Rear panel

BELL COBRA

AH-IT (TOW)
Front panel (TSU deleted
for clarity)

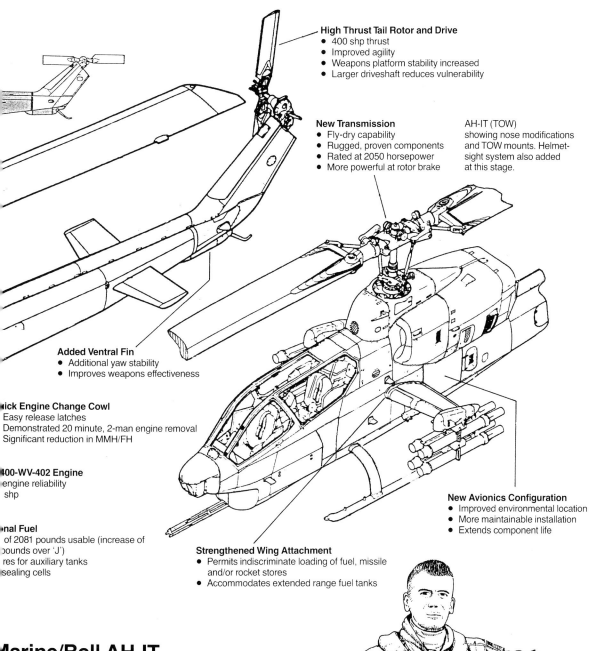

High Thrust Tail Rotor and Drive
- 400 shp thrust
- Improved agility
- Weapons platform stability increased
- Larger driveshaft reduces vulnerability

New Transmission
- Fly-dry capability
- Rugged, proven components
- Rated at 2050 horsepower
- More powerful at rotor brake

AH-IT (TOW)
showing nose modifications
and TOW mounts. Helmet-
sight system also added
at this stage.

Added Ventral Fin
- Additional yaw stability
- Improves weapons effectiveness

▪ick Engine Change Cowl
Easy release latches
Demonstrated 20 minute, 2-man engine removal
Significant reduction in MMH/FH

▪00-WV-402 Engine
engine reliability
shp

▪nal Fuel
of 2081 pounds usable (increase of
▪ounds over 'J')
res for auxiliary tanks
sealing cells

Strengthened Wing Attachment
- Permits indiscriminate loading of fuel, missile
  and/or rocket stores
- Accommodates extended range fuel tanks

New Avionics Configuration
- Improved environmental location
- More maintainable installation
- Extends component life

Marine/Bell AH-IT
Features

Typical Tango pilot
with HGU-54/P with 'monocle'
for HSS, and snap rings
intended to fasten pilot
to another Cobra's gun-bay
door in the event of an
emergency extraction
being required

Fig 8

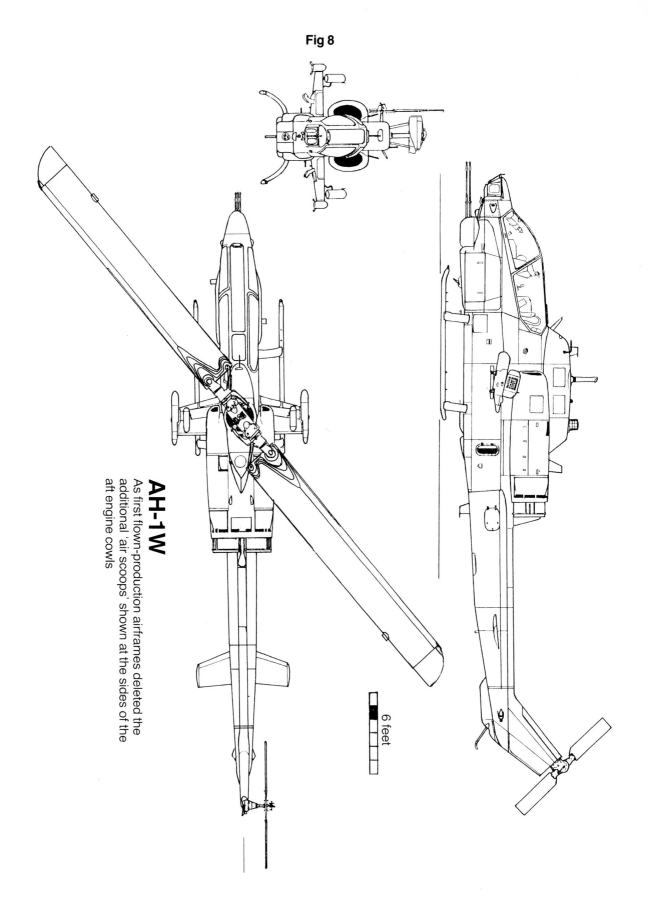

AH-1W

As first flown-production airframes deleted the additional 'air scoops' shown at the sides of the aft engine cowls

6 feet

Fig 9

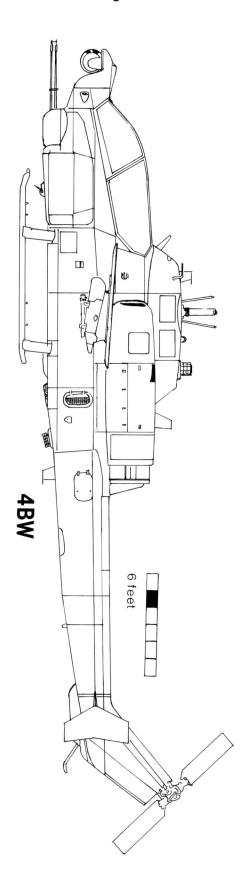

4BW

6 feet

reportedly on similar machines destined for South Korea. The Japanese camouflage was originally compromised by bold white markings, but these have now been removed in favour of a more sensible 'low-vis' presentation.

US Marine Corps
Early machines for the USMC were painted overall in their distinctive gloss, Field green 14097. Full national insignia, with white MARINES and serial presentation were standard, as was a yellow (13538) tail rotor warning band. The tail skid was often striped red and yellow, and the cockpit interiors were all Dark gull gray.

With the onset of the 'low-vis' movement after the Vietnam War, all USMC Cobras went into drab colours. The high gloss finish was replaced with matt Field green (34095), and all markings, including a now rather skeletal national insignia, were rendered in matt black. Due to the salt-laden atmosphere of a marine environment, the finish invariably weathered badly, and the overall effect was often characterized by much retouching.

In around 1980, at least two AH-1Ts at Camp Pendleton were finished in a scheme reminiscent of the Army's pattern painting ideas. They apparently looked most attractive, but sadly we have been unable to find sufficient detail to include an accurate drawing.

The Marines have recently decided to standardize on a three-colour 'wraparound' scheme, consisting of green 34095, gray 35237 and black 37038. All AH-1W aircraft are now leaving the factory finished in this way, and the AH-1Js are progressively being repainted in the same scheme. Fig 14 shows an example of each pattern.

Foreign operators
SPAIN The AH-1Gs supplied to Spain were painted overall in two coats of Sea blue gloss 15042.

IRAN Fig 15. Originally the Iranian scheme, which uses standard 'Asia Minor' colours, consisted of Brown 30140 and Tan 20400 topsides, with Gray 36622 on the underside. On later aircraft the gray was omitted, and the brown and tan extended underneath the fuselage.

ISRAEL Fig 15. Cobras for this most secretive of nations leave the factory in an overall finish which is supplied to Bell by the Israeli Government. It is known in the Paint Shop as 'Israeli Tan', and is very close to 30140 in colour.

JORDAN Fig 16. At last a different colour for the AH-1S! This very attractive scheme again features the 'Asia Minor' colours of 30140 and 20400, but this time in combination with Green 34097. The wingtips and extreme nose look black, but they are actually painted in the US Army's Aircraft green.

KOREA All the original AH-1Js supplied to South Korea were finished overall in Olive drab 34087.

Fig 10

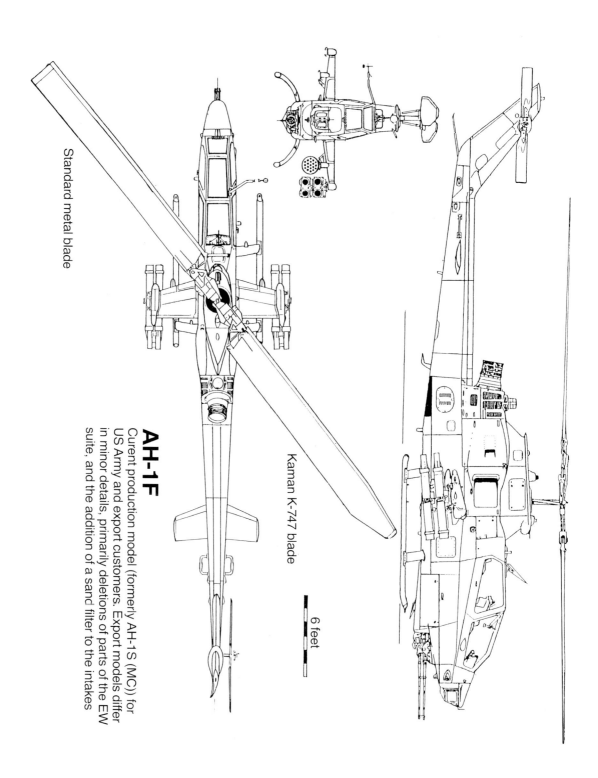

Standard metal blade

Kaman K-747 blade

6 feet

AH-1F

Curent production model (formerly AH-1S (MC)) for US Army and export customers. Export models differ in minor details, primarily deletions of parts of the EW suite, and the addition of a sand filter to the intakes

Fig 11

AH-1F

Instrument and electronics
Typical layout

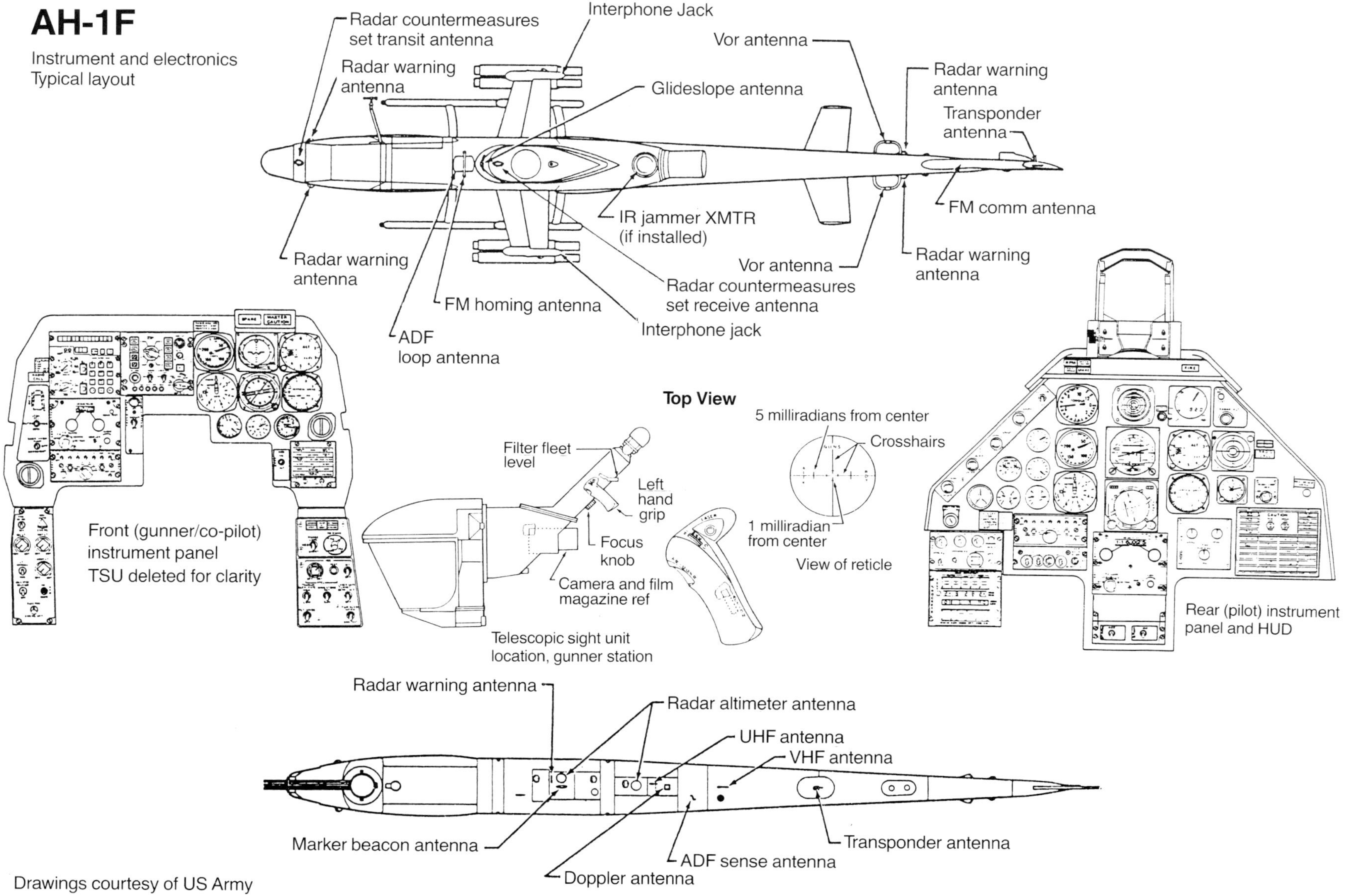

Front (gunner/co-pilot)
instrument panel
TSU deleted for clarity

Radar countermeasures
set transit antenna

Radar warning
antenna

Radar warning
antenna

ADF
loop antenna

FM homing antenna

Interphone Jack

Interphone
set receive antenna

Radar countermeasures
set receive antenna

Vor antenna

IR jammer XMTR
(if installed)

Glideslope antenna

Interphone Jack

Vor antenna

Top View

Filter fleet
level

Focus
knob

Left
hand
grip

Camera and film
magazine ref

Telescopic sight unit
location, gunner station

Radar warning antenna

Marker beacon antenna

Doppler antenna

ADF sense antenna

Transponder antenna

VHF antenna

UHF antenna

Radar altimeter antenna

Radar warning antenna

Radar warning
antenna

FM comm antenna

Transponder
antenna

Radar warning
antenna

1 milliradian
from center

5 milliradians from center

Crosshairs

View of reticle

Rear (pilot) instrument
panel and HUD

183

Fig 12

Comparative Data (Bell figures for Cobra variants)		AH-1G	AH-1J (USMC)	AH-1J (International or Iran) with TOW	AH-1S (MC) (K-747 rotor)	AH-1T with TOW
Length overall (rotors turning)		53' (16.14 m)	53'5" (16.29 m)		53' (16.14 m)	58' (17.68 m)
Fuselage length		44'5" (13.53 m)	44'7" (13.58 m)			45'7" (13.90 m)*
Wingspan		10'4" (3.15 m)		10'9" (3.28 m) ††		
Elevator span		6'11" (2.12 m)				
Rotor (main)	Diameter	44' (13.41 m)				48' (14.63 m)
	Chord	2'3" (0.69 m)			2'6" (0.76 m)	2'9" (0.84 m)
Rotor (tail)	Diameter	8'6" (2.6 m)				9'9" (2.95 m)
	Chord	8½" (0.21 m)	1' (0.30 m)		11½" (0.27 m)	1' (0.30 m)
Weights	Empty	5809 lb (2634 kg)	6610 lb (2998 kg)	6899 lb (3129 kg)	6598 lb (2992 kg) †	8553 lb (3879 kg)
	Gross	9500 lb (4309 kg)	10,000 lb (4536 kg)			14,000 lb (6350 kg)
Speed	Max (VNE)	230 mph (370 km/h) ‡	207 mph (333 km/h)		195 mph (315 km/h)	
	Cruise max	190 mph (305 km/h) ‡			141 mph (227 km/h)	154 mph (247 km/h)
Engine	Manufacturer	Lycoming	United Aircraft of Canada	United Aircraft of Canada	Lycoming	United Aircraft of Canada
	Designation	T-53-L-13	Twin-Pac T400-CP-400	Twin-Pac T400-WV-402	T53-L-703	Twin-Pac T400-WV-402
	Horse power	1400 shp	1800 shp	1970 shp	1800 shp	1970 shp

† Basic aircraft. Added equipment places current aircraft around 7000 lb.

†† Including TOW launchers

* Fuselage lengthened by 3'7" insert (total) but cut down of fin reduces total by 2'5"

** Gunship configuration

‡ Prototype clean – see J or S for representative figures

AH-1W	Kingcobra	YAH-63	AH-64 Apache	AH-56 Cheyenne	S-67 Blackhawk
	59'3" (18.06 m)	69'8½" (21.20 m)	58'2" (17.73 m)	60'3" (18.31 m)	74'1" (22.58 m)
	48'9" (14.86 m)	60'9" (18.52 m)	49'6"	51'9"	64'2" (19.56 m)
	13' (3.96 m) ⋆	17'11" (5.47 m)	17'2" (5.23 m)	26'8½" (8.14 m)	27'4" (8.33 m)
		N/A	11'2" (3.40 m)	11'	15'10" (4.82 m)
		51'6" (15.70 m)	48' (14.63 m)	50'4¾" (15.36 m)	62' (18.9 m)
		3'6" (1.06 m)	1'9"	2'3" (0.69 m)	
	10'2" (3.10 m)	9'6" (2.90 m)	9'9½" (2.795 m)	9'	10'7" (3.26 m)
		1'5" (0.42 m)	9"	1' (0.30 m)	
8000 lb (est)	8926 lb (4048 kg)		10,759 lb (4880 kg)	11,725 lb (5323 kg)	12,514 lb (5681 kg)
14,000 lb (6350 kg)	15,000 lb (6804 kg)	19,224 lb (8734 kg)	18,352 lb (8324 kg)	22,000 lb (9988 kg)	14,000 lb (6356 kg)**
	230 mph (370 km/h)	197 mph (317 km/h)	235 mph (378 km/h)	253 mph	193 mph (311 km/h)
183 mph (294 km/h)			182 mph (293 km/h)	242 mph (389 km/h)	187 mph (301 km/h)
General Electric	United Aircraft of Canada / Ship 2 Lycoming	General Electric	General Electric	General Electric	General Electric
T700-GE-401 (x2)	T400-CP-400 / T55-L-7C	T700-GE-700 (x2)	T700-GE-700 (x2)	T64-GE-16	T58-GE-5 (x2)
1625 shp each	1970 shp / 2850 shp	1596 shp each	1536 shp each	3435 shp	1500 shp each
	Similar and connected types				

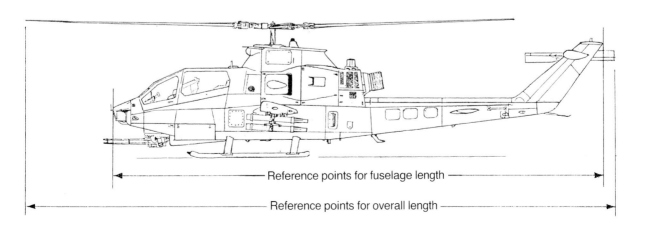

Reference points for fuselage length

Reference points for overall length

Fig 13

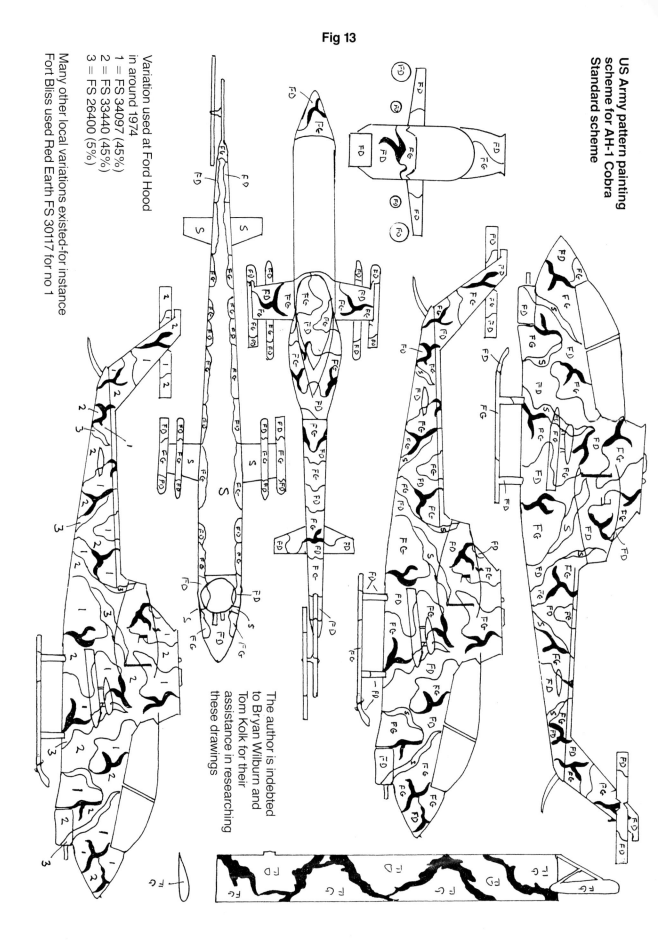

US Army pattern painting scheme for AH-1 Cobra
Standard scheme

Variation used at Ford Hood in around 1974

1 = FS 34097 (45%)
2 = FS 33440 (45%)
3 = FS 26400 (5%)

Many other local variations existed-for instance Fort Bliss used Red Earth FS 30117 for no 1

The author is indebted to Bryan Wilburn and Tom Kolk for their assistance in researching these drawings

Fig 14

USMC current scheme

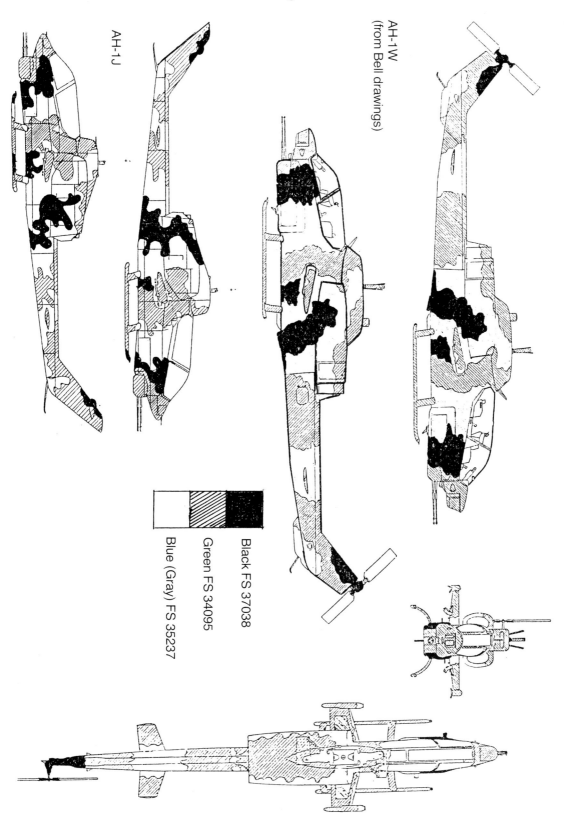

AH-1J

AH-1W
(from Bell drawings)

Black FS 37038

Green FS 34095

Blue (Gray) FS 35237

Fig 15

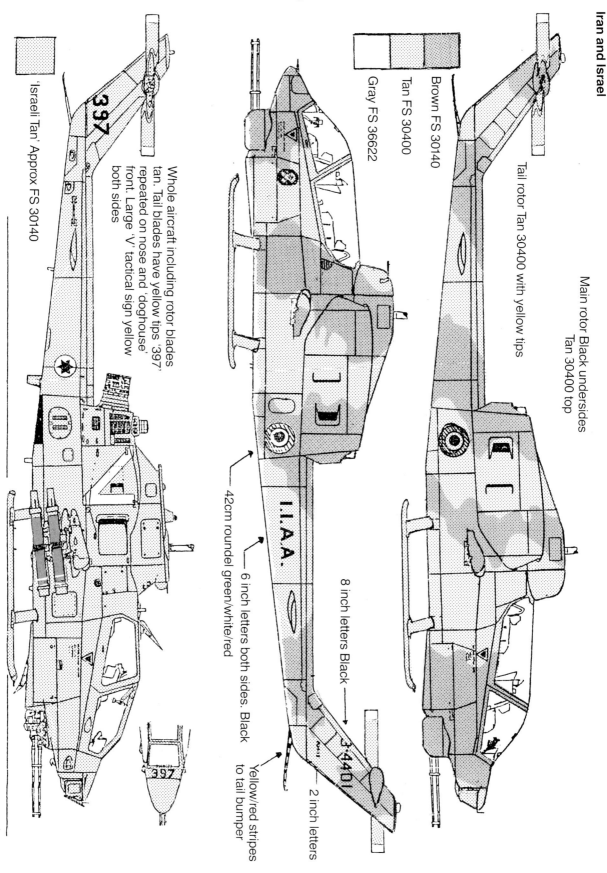

Brown FS 30140

Tan FS 30400

Gray FS 36622

Tail rotor Tan 30400 with yellow tips

Main rotor Black undersides
Tan 30400 top

42cm roundel green/white/red

6 inch letters both sides. Black

8 inch letters Black

I.I.A.A.

Yellow/red stripes
to tail bumper

2 inch letters

'Israeli Tan' Approx FS 30140

Whole aircraft including rotor blades
tan. Tail blades have yellow tips. '397'
repeated on nose and 'doghouse'
front. Large 'V' tactical sign yellow
both sides

397

397

Fig 16

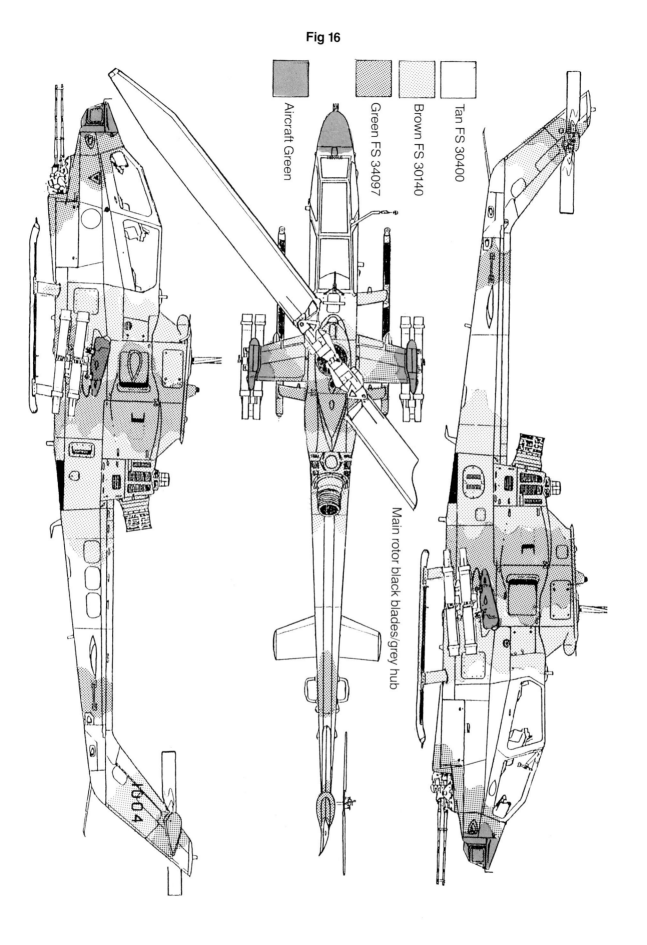

Aircraft Green

Green FS 34097

Brown FS 30140

Tan FS 30400

Main rotor black blades/grey hub

Fig 17

Parent ship USS Guam (LPH-9) aircraft details c February 1984 off Beirut coast

Basic Colour notes

1 Aircraft is overall Field green FS 34097
2 All makings, stencils, main rotor and skids are black
3 Tail rotor Olive drab FS 34087, tips Yellow FS 13538
4 Cockpit interior Dark gull gray FS 36231
5 National insignia 15 inches diameter
6 'Marines' in 10 inch letters. BuNo and Sqn code 8 inch letters.
  AH-1T (under BuNo) 2 inch letters
7 Sharkmouth and name were 'cruise only' and unofficial added en route to
  Lebanon, as were 'kills'

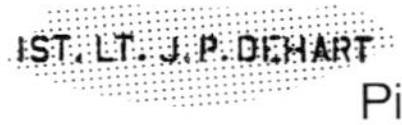

Armament standard load

Station	Weapon	Marking	Use
4 (outer port)	4 x 5 inch Zuni pod/proximity fuse		Air-to-air
3	4 x 5 inch Zuni pod/point detonating fuse		Air-to-surface
2	7 x 2.75 FFAR Pod/WP	Marking	
1	4 x TOW missiles		Air-to-surface

Note HMM 261
'Snorting bull'
emblem both cowl
sides

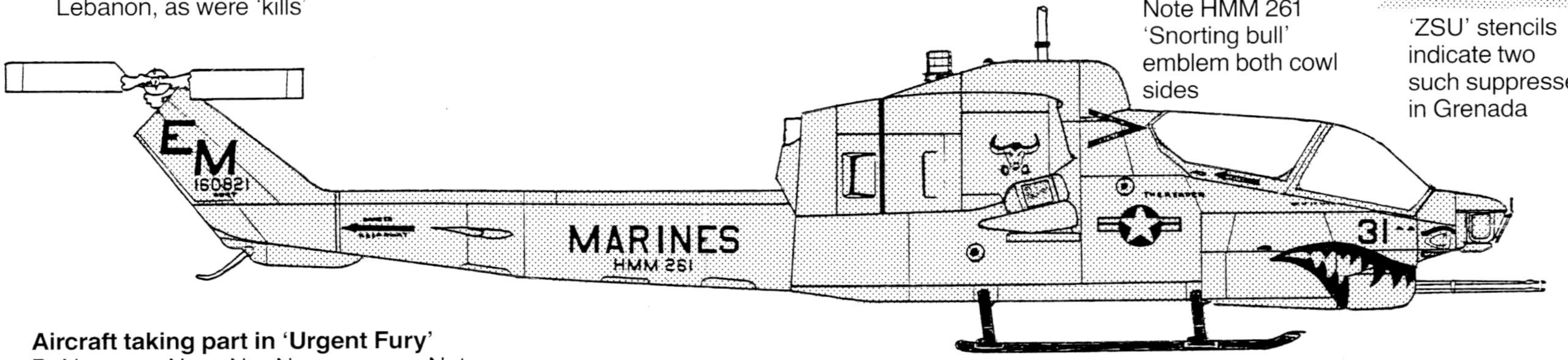

Pilot's name
below cockpit

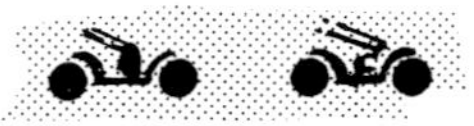

IST. LT. J. P. DEHART

'ZSU' stencils
indicate two
such suppressed
in Grenada

MARINES
HMM 261

THE REAPER

Aircraft name positioned above and ahead
of national insignia on both sides

Aircraft taking part in 'Urgent Fury'

BuNo	Nose No	Name	Notes
160112	32		
160812	30		shot down on the same day
160747	33	El Tigre	Shot down 23.10.83. Pilot, Capt JF Seagle awarded posthumous Navy Cross for saving co-pilot
160821	31	The Reaper	
160816	3?	Leviathan	replacement
160817	3?		replacement

Back to the drawing board

This section represents an opportunity to look at some projects which, although they did not make it into production, proved useful to later developments.

OVERLEAF, TOP
Very little is known about the 'Night Striker' Cobra of June 1968. Both main and tail rotors have the swept tips later used on the KingCobra prototypes, and the cockpit area appears to have additional Ausform-type armour panels. Probably of more significance is the bigger, more rounded nose profile (containing a moving target indicator) and the clearly 'different' turret arrangement. This appears to contain a FLIR/LLTV type sensor, or a NiteSun searchlight, mounted directly alongside the gun. Both configurations would have made sense for base perimeter defences in Vietnam, but it seems doubtful that either combination would have remained operational for long because of the intense vibration levels involved. The under wing armament appears to consist of M-18 gun pods (outboard) and rocket launchers (Bell)

BELOW
Normally a shoulder-fired infantry weapon, this General Dynamics coupled Redeye anti-aircraft missile system was tried briefly on a USMC AH-1J Cobra. The Redeye was not a success, but its installation paved the way for the subsequent fitting of Sidewinders, and it now seems possible that the much lighter Stinger missile will be used in the future (Bell)

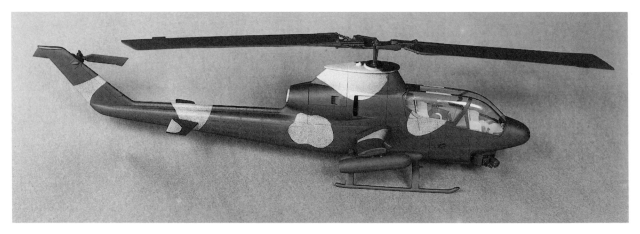

BELOW
Dating from early 1971, the 'Flip-Tip' Cobra was an interesting scheme to increase the speed and weight-carrying capabilities of the aircraft—initially by providing a wide-track, wheeled undercarriage to allow 'rolling' take-offs, and then by increasing the wing area to off-load the rotor. Note the return of the ventral fin, and the small, castoring tailwheel. The idea was abandoned at an early stage (Bell)

PRECEDING PAGE, ABOVE
*Another seemingly unrecorded project is this Model 280
'wide body' Cobra. It appears to have been based on the
twin-engined AH-1J and carries a pseudo-71 USAF serial
over the then standard SE Asia camouflage. Its turreted
gun and long-range tanks suggest that it might have been
designed as a combat-rescue vehicle, intended to pull downed
aircrew out of hostile territory* (Bell)

PRECEDING PAGE, BELOW
*This AH-1J (157769) was used extensively in support of
the AH-1W programme. Apart from the obvious
Sidewinders, the aircraft is seen here fitted with radar
jammers and laser-scan detectors. Its front and rear cockpits
are shown in the colour section* (HMLA-167)

ABOVE
*The Cobra prototype was originally flown with a large
ventral fin and a retractable skid undercarriage: neither of
these features was carried through onto production aircraft*
(Bell)

Glossary

AAA	'Triple-A', Anti-aircraft artillery		Requirement for Equipment for HueyCobra programme
AAFSS	'Ayfuss' Advanced Aerial Fire Support System	FAC	Forward Air Control
AAH	Advanced Attack Helicopter	FARP	Forward Arming and Refuelling Point
AGI	Soviet intelligence-gathering ship		
AGM	Air-to-Ground Missile	FEBA	Forward Edge of Battle Area
AHIP	Army Helicopter Improvement Program	FFAR	Forward-firing Aerial Rocket
		FLIR	Forward-looking-Infra-red
ALLD	Airborne Laser Locator/Designator	HARM	High-speed, Anti-radiation Missile
ARTI	Advanced Rotorcraft Technology Integration Program	HE	High Explosive
		HEAT	High Explosive Anti-Tank warhead for FFARs
ASH	Advanced Scout Helicopter		
ATAFCS	Airborne Target Acquisition Fire Control System	HEI	High Explosive Incendiary
		HSS	Helmet Sighting System
Bear	Tupolev Tu-95	HUD	Head-up Display
BITE	Built-in Test Equipment	ICAM	Improved Cobra Agility and Maneuverability programme
CAS	Combat Air Strike Forward Air		
FAC(A)	Control (Aircraft)	ICAP	Improved Cobra Armament Program
CDEC	US Army's Combat Development Experimental Command	IHADSS	Integrated Helmet and Display Sighting Sub-system
CEP	Circular Error Probable is a measure of the expected accuracy of ballistic weapons. Expressed as a distance, it describes the radius of a circle, into which 50 per cent of the rounds fired at the centre of the circle will consistently fall. Obviously the better the aiming system, the smaller the circle will be.	IIR	Imaging Infra-red
		INS	Inertial Navigation System
		JAAT	Joint Air Attack Team
		JCS	Joint Chiefs of Staff
		KIA	Killed in Action
		LHX	Light Helicopter Experimental
		LLTV	Low-light Television
		LPH	Amphibious transport dock—assault ship
CIFS	Computer-Interactive Flight Simulation		
		LZ	Landing Zone
CONFICS	Cobra Night Fire Control System	MAAG	Military Assistance Advisory Group
DZ	Drop Zone	MARHUK	MARine HUnter Killer operation during Vietnam War
ECAS	Enhanced Cobra Armament System		
ECM	Electronic Countermeasures	MAW	Marine Aircraft Wing
ENSURE	Expedite Non-Standard Urgent	MRAM	Medium Range Attack Missile
		NETT	New Equipment Training Team

NOE	Nap of Earth flying	SMS	Stabilized Multi-sensor Sight
NPE	Navy Preliminary Evaluation	SSPI	Sighting Station Passive Infra-red
NVG	Night Vision Goggles	TADS/	Target Acquisition and Designation
RABFAC	Radar Beacon Forward Air Control	PNVS	Sight/Pilot's Night Vision Sensor
RADHAZ	RADiation HAZard	TARPS	Tactical Aircraft Reconnaissance Pod
RFP	Request for Proposals		System
RWR	Radar Warning Receiver	TOW	Hughes Tube-launched, Optically-
SAM	Surface-to-Air Missile		tracked, Wire-guided anti-armour
SAR	Search and Rescue		missile
SCAS	Stability Control Augmentation	TSU	Telescopic Sight Unit
	System	VNE	Velocity never to be exceeded in any
SCAT	Scout/Attack Helicopter		particular type of aircraft
SMASH	SE Asia Multi-sensor Armament	WIA	Wounded in Action
	Sub-system for HueyCobra	WP	White Phosphorus
	programme	WSPS	Wire Strike Protection System

Select Bibliography

Bell publications

Bell Helicopter News (various issues)
Helicopter Reference data (various editions)
History of Model 209, November 1972
History of Model 309 KingCobra, September 1980
Kelly, Bartram, transcript of the twelfth Cierva
    Memorial Lecture
Seibel, Charles, *US Army HueyCobra configuration
    and design considerations*, May 1967
——, *YAH-63 AAH configuration: Design
    considerations and development status*, May 1975

UK Ministry of Defence publications

Army Aviation Centre *Trials Report No 136*

US Army publications

TM-55-1520-236-10 (AH-1 operator's manual)
US Army Aviation Digest
Vanderpool, Colonel Jay D, 'We armed the
    helicopter', *US Army Aviation Digest*

US Marine Corps publications

Marines and helicopters 1962–73
The Marines in Vietnam 1954–73
US Marines in Vietnam 1954–64
US Marines in Vietnam 1965
US Marines in Vietnam 1966
US Marines in Vietnam 1967

Various Command Chronologies and Reports
    including
HML-367 Jan/Feb/Mar/Apr 1971
HMA-369 Jan to Dec 1971

General

Drendel, Lou, *Air War over Southeast Asia* (3 vols),
    Sqn/Signal publications
——, *Gunslingers in Action*, Sqn/Signal publications
——, *Huey*, Sqn/Signal publications
Mesco, Jim, *Airmobile*, Sqn/Signal publications
Miller, J, *Aerophile 2/2*, Miller
Polmar and Kennedy, *Military Helicopters of the
    World*, Arms & Armour Press
US Military Aircraft Serials, SEEFIVE
    Publications

Periodicals and Magazines

Air Enthusiast International
Aviation News★
Defence Helicopter World
Flight International
Flying Review International
IPMS UK magazine★
IPMS US magazine★
Koku Fan★
Scale Aircraft Modelling★

(★ contains details of colour schemes)

Index

BELL AIRCRAFT

Cobra variants